THE IRISH FARMERS' MARKET COOKBOOK

THE IRISH FARMERS' MARKET COOKBOOK

Clodagh McKenna

Photography by Jean Cazals

Collins

Contents

Introduction

I first heard about farmers' markets when I was working as a chef at Ballymaloe House. There was a lot of talk in the kitchens about Midleton Market, and the creative, passionate producers who were selling fantastic cheeses and artisan foods. I was, to say the least, curious. My big chance to get involved with the market came when Myrtle Allen, proprietor of Ballymaloe House (an incredible guest house with an award-winning restaurant), asked me to look after her stall selling freshly baked breads one very cold Saturday before Christmas. The atmosphere was buzzing; the stall holders were so enthusiastic, so keen to tell you about their produce, how it was made, the best way to cook and eat it, how to store it and where they sourced ingredients. These people were connected to the food they were sourcing, making and selling. They knew every detail, down to the name of the person who grew the herbs they used to cure the bacon in the smokehouse, and the type of wood they used and exactly where they got it. Try asking those questions in your local supermarket! There was a feeling of the stall holders being part of an underground food revolution and by the end of that freezing day I was completely hooked.

So, I got myself a stall. I would finish service at Ballymaloe on a Friday night and go right to work making fresh pasta for the market. I'd be at the market by 8am, sell it all by midday, pack up, and be back at Ballymaloe in time for service at 2pm. People thought I was completely mad but I was on a high! I left Ballymaloe about six months later to do the markets full time. For the following three years my life consisted of making produce to sell at my stall and kick-starting other markets around the country.

I feel passionately that good food should be available to everyone. Our Irish food culture is very much alive but needs to grow. For that to happen we need to buy and consume Irish produce from farmers' markets so that we can be sure the money goes back into the industry and not into the pockets of multinational supermarket chains. The farmers' markets are not just for 'foodies' – they are for all of us. Further benefits of the farmers' markets include:

- The food hasn't travelled several thousand miles so it is fresher and you are helping the planet by saving food miles.
- The food is seasonal, picked for optimum flavour and nutritional value.

- It puts you, the consumer, back in touch with the producer, so you know where your food is coming from and how it was produced.
- There is a fantastic range of produce available: meats; smoked and fresh fish; a staggering range of dairy produce, particularly cheese; artisan breads; preserves; ready meals; oils and, of course, fruit and vegetables.
- Some of our greatest producers have stalls at the farmers' markets; such as Sheridan cheesemongers, Ballymaloe Cookery School, Gubbeen Farmhouse Products and Belvelly Smokehouse to name just a few.
- You will be putting money back into the community.
- You will be keeping Irish cultural and culinary traditions alive.

Artisan producers and farmers' markets have revitalised local rural economies, providing employment and attracting younger generations back in droves. The government is desperate to find a way to encourage young generations to stay on family farms, and these local traditions provide fantastic opportunities. Top chefs are beating a path to stall holders to get the best produce, and tourists are flocking to buy and taste locally produced food, so this is clearly an industry worth supporting and encouraging.

So why is it that the government doesn't take the farmers' markets seriously? Why doesn't it get involved with the markets and support artisan producers? Why isn't the government working alongside the producers to come up with regulations that meet the producers' needs as well as adhere to legislative requirements? The way to show the government how serious we are about our food culture is to support it by using the farmers' markets.

The markets have reunited us with producers and given us back a connection with the food we are consuming. I've written this book as a celebration of all the fantastic produce we have in Ireland and as an encouragement for others to start searching out their local markets. The recipes are a guide for what can be cooked at home using local and seasonal produce. If you don't happen to live in Ireland, seek out your local market and ask the producers to suggest substitutes for produce that you may not be able to get. The best lesson that I ever learned as a chef was that if you use the best of local and seasonal ingredients you can't go too far wrong. Plus, nothing is more rewarding than sitting at home with your family around the kitchen table, talking about where your food came from and looking at the delight on their faces as they take their first bite. I have written profiles of my favourite producers who have changed my idea of food and who have helped create this Irish food revolution. I hope that it gives you an insight into these fabulous characters. You will also find lots of useful information at the back of this book: recommendations of places to eat, how to find the markets and how to contact the producers. I hope this book opens your eyes to the wonderful produce we have in Ireland, just as the last six years have done for me....

The Irish Farmers' Market Cookbook

What is Slow Food?

Many of the food products sold at farmers' markets are from artisan producers who are members of the Slow Food movement, which was started by Italian philosopher Carlo Petrini. He wanted to educate people about the great tradition of artisan food production that still thrives in the Italian countryside. Petrini saw young Italians queuing outside a notorious fast-food burger joint and it occurred to him if people knew about great artisan food, if they tasted the difference, they might just choose to eat it instead.

By celebrating and promoting artisan produce, Slow Food ensures that these delicious foods continue to be enjoyed and are not lost under an avalanche of standardisation, bureaucratic hygienics and over-commercialisation.

Slow Food now has chapters in 40 different countries. In Ireland, it acts as a lively umbrella organisation for our artisan producers, entrepreneurs and, increasingly, for consumers who care about methods of production, traceability, quality, and who agree with the 'buy local, fresh and seasonal' message. Here are a few more reasons to join us at Slow Food:

- Slow Food is about taking the time to put good food first; the time to grow it, the time to prepare it, and the time to sit down with family and friends and enjoy it.
- Slow Food is the antidote to fast food. In the face of over-commercialisation and homogenisation we make people aware of the rich tradition of artisan food production.
- Slow Food promotes the awareness of artisan food production and farmers' markets.
- Slow Food supports artisan producers who are being suffocated by overly stringent EU rules and regulations.
- Slow Food is working to educate the next generation about Irish Food and its production.

Pictured left: A stall holder takes a break in her Slow Food Ireland apron.

How to Use This Book

All the recipes in this book are based on ingredients you'll find at farmers' markets. I choose to buy free range or organic produce, but what do these terms mean? Put simply, 'free range' refers to meat, poultry and game that has been allowed to roam outside, rather than raised in contained areas. 'Organic' means that the food has been produced to set specifications and without the use of synthetic chemicals, such as fertilisers, pesticides, antibiotics or hormones. Rather confusingly, products can be both organic and free range. One of the great reasons for buying at the markets is that you can talk to the stall holders and find out exactly how the food has been produced.

You may wish to take this book with you when you go shopping. When you first get to your farmers' market have a walk around and see what is available, then flick through the book and see what recipes you could make. If you decided, for example, that you want to make the Aubergine and Goat's Cheese Rolls (see page 113) then ask at the cheese stall what local soft goat's cheeses are available. Once you are feeling confident with this book, try adding your own alternatives. But always remember the producers at the farmers' markets are experts in their field and will only be too happy to help you with alternatives and suggestions.

Cooking with an Aga

I adore my Aga – I love the way it breathes life into my kitchen. Agas are perfect for making slow-cooked food that brings the family together.

The recipes in this book are given in conventional oven temperatures (Celsius, Fahrenheit and Gas Mark), but if you cook with an Aga, as I do, here is a handy conversion chart:

CONVENTIONAL OVEN	FAN OVEN	FAHRENHEIT	GAS MARK	AGA 2 OVEN	AGA 3 & 4 OVEN
150°C	130°C	300°F	2	Simmering oven	Simmering oven
170°C	150°C	325°F	3	Grid shelf on floor of roasting oven and cold plain shelf above	Grid shelf on floor of baking oven
180°C	160°C	350°F	4	Grid shelf on floor of roasting oven and cold plain shelf above	Lowest runner of baking oven
190°C	170°C	375°F	5	Grid shelf on floor of roasting oven	Top of baking oven
200°C	180°C	400°F	6	Lowest set of runners in roasting oven	Lowest set of runners in roasting oven
220°C	200°C	425°F	7	3rd or 4th set of runners in roasting oven	3rd or 4th set of runners in roasting oven

Bread

An Irish Staple

Really good bread is a healthy, easily digestible, source of energy and one of the most nutritionally balanced foods available. It is full of carbohydrate, fibre, protein, calcium and B vitamins. I don't mean the supermarket loaves that stick to the back of your teeth and line your stomach like glue. I mean great artisan bread with a beautiful texture, made from the finest flour and baked with true skill and care.

There is a world of difference in the taste and nutritional value of a good loaf and a bad one. So what makes the difference? The answer lies in the flour used, the milling and the way the bread is baked. Wheat grain is made up of bran (the outer layer), the endosperm, which contains the starch, and the germ, which contains the proteins, vitamins, oil and most of the flavour. When flour is stone ground it is a relatively gentle process that leaves most of the nutrients intact. Flour was ground this way for centuries before two things happened: white bread and mass production. Refined white flour might make better looking bread, but most of the goodness is extracted. The large factories that now produce 80% of our bread use a system that does an enormous amount of grinding under huge pressure. The flour ends up fractured and absorbs water like a sponge, which the factories love because water provides volume and weight. This system also uses double the yeast to make up for the short fermentation time, which makes the bread less digestible. Then there are the high levels of salt added to enhance the flavour, not to mention the additives, the improvers, the genetically modified enzymes, the hydrogenated fat, the preservatives ... This cheap mass-produced white sliced bread is as nutritionally valuable as your inner sole.

The good news is we have always had a great tradition of quality bakers in Ireland. You will be astounded by the variety of artisan breads available at the farmers' markets. Declan Ryan, who runs Arbutus Bakery, is typical of the passionate, skilled brigade of dedicated artisan bakers selling their loaves at the farmers' markets. He uses the finest French and Irish stone-ground flours to produce a range of West Cork soda bread, rye, wholemeal, white sourdough and continental breads. Everything is hand-kneaded and slow-proofed to make crusty, chewy, flavoursome breads. And that's what sorts the wheat from the chaff: passion, skill, care and respect for the ingredients. When you've eaten a really good loaf you won't go back, and with so much choice you won't have to.

Irish Soda Bread
(or Cake, as it is known in Ireland)

Soda bread was traditionally known in Ireland as soda 'cake' as it contains buttermilk. Traditionally this was a luxury ingredient and therefore would be served as a treat. During festive times, fruit would be added to the mixture. This is the easiest bread recipe that I have ever baked and is still my favourite! It bakes especially well in an Aga.

Makes 1 loaf
450g (1lb) wholemeal flour
450g (1lb) white flour
1½ tsp bread soda or
    bicarbonate of soda
1 tsp salt
600 ml (1 pint) buttermilk
    or sour milk

Sieve the flours, soda and salt into a large bowl and make a hollow in the centre. Gradually pour in the buttermilk (or sour milk, see tip), mixing to form a dough.

Pat your hands with flour and shape the dough into one round. Place on a floured baking tray. Flour a large knife and cut the shape of a cross into the top of the dough about two-thirds of the way through, and then stab every quarter with the knife. This old Irish tradition was used to kill the fairies!

Bake in a preheated oven at 220°C, 425°F, Gas Mark 7 for about 25 minutes, then turn the bread over for a further 5 minutes. To test whether the loaf is cooked, tap the back with your knuckles; it should sound hollow. Leave to cool on a cooling rack.

Tip: If you are unable to get your hands on buttermilk or sour milk, you can add 2 teaspoons cream of tartar to the bread soda. Add this to the flour, then mix in half fresh milk and half water and continue as above.

White Soda Scones with Cheese and Thyme

This delicious savoury scone recipe is fantastic served with soup. If you wish, try omitting the thyme and add some sun-dried tomatoes.

Makes 8 scones
225g (8oz) strong white flour
1 tbsp baking powder
pinch of sea salt
50g (2oz) butter
125g (4 1/2 oz) mature Cheddar
    cheese, grated (e.g.
    Hegarty's or Bandon Vale)
1 tsp chopped fresh thyme
125–150ml (4 1/2 –5fl oz) milk

Sieve the flour, baking powder and sea salt into a bowl. Rub the butter into the flour mixture until it resembles fine breadcrumbs. Stir in two-thirds of the grated cheese, followed by the thyme. Gradually pour in sufficient milk to make a soft dough.

Roll out the dough on a floured surface to a thickness of 1cm (1/2in). Cut into circles with a pastry cutter or an upturned glass. Place the circles on an oiled baking tray and sprinkle with the remaining cheese.

Bake in a preheated oven at 200°C, 400°F, Gas Mark 6 for 12–15 minutes. Transfer to a cooling rack for 5 minutes, then eat hot with lashings of Glenilen country butter – yum!

Short Scones with Glenilen Clotted Cream and Rhubarb

Glenilen is a wonderful dairy farm in West Cork run and owned by Valerie and Alan Kingston. They make the most delicious clotted cream, yogurts, butter and crème fraîche from the milk off their herd.

If you love shortbread and scones equally, then you are going to adore this recipe as it is a combination of the two. It can be served for brunch, afternoon tea or even dessert.

Serves 8
300g (10oz) plain flour
50g (2oz) caster sugar
1 tsp baking powder
130g (4½oz) butter, cold
   from the fridge
1 egg
100ml (3½fl oz) single
   cream
beaten egg, for brushing
   (optional)

For the filling:
500g (1lb 2oz) rhubarb,
   cut into 2.5cm (1in)
   pieces
150g (5oz) caster sugar
50ml (2fl oz) water
200ml (7fl oz) Glenilen
   clotted cream

Prepare the filling. Place the rhubarb in an ovenproof dish and cover with the sugar and water. Cook in a preheated oven at 170°C, 325°F, Gas Mark 3 for about 30 minutes or until the rhubarb is tender.

To make the short scones, mix the flour, sugar and baking powder in a bowl. Grate in the butter and mix together. Beat the egg and cream in a separate bowl and stir into the flour mixture.

Pat both hands with flour and transfer the dough to a floured surface. Roll out the dough, about 2.5cm (1in) thick, and cut out 8 rounds. Brush lightly with some beaten egg (optional) and chill in the fridge for 1 hour.

Transfer to a lightly floured baking tray and cook in a preheated oven at 220°C, 425°F, Gas Mark 7 for 10 minutes or until lightly golden brown. Leave the scones to cool a little before splitting them open, while they are still warm, and filling with the stewed rhubarb and a big dollop of Glenilen clotted cream.

Kaitlin's Mini Focaccias

This recipe was given to me by a good friend of mine, Kaitlin Ruth, who I met at the Clonakilty market. She used to have a stall near mine and would sell out of these focaccias in an hour! She now runs the kitchen at Deasy's Bar in Ring and has turned it into the biggest food destination in West Cork. She's living proof that all good things come from farmers' markets!

Makes 6

4 tbsp fresh yeast
85g (3oz) caster sugar
1.2ml (2 pints) warm water
1.75kg (4lb) strong white flour
4 tsp salt
90ml (3fl oz) olive oil

Choose one of these topping combinations:

1 caramelised red onion and 50g (2oz) Gubbeen cheese (or a semi-soft cheese of your choice), diced into small cubes

2 tbsp toasted pumpkin seeds, 4 jalapeño peppers (finely sliced), 8 sprigs fresh coriander and 50g (2oz) grated Cheddar cheese

60g (2oz) roasted pumpkin and 40g (1¼ oz) grated Desmond cheese (or Parmesan cheese)

16 semi sun-dried tomatoes and 50g (2oz) Durrus (or a raw milk cheese of your choice), diced into small cubes

Place the fresh yeast and caster sugar in a large bowl and then whisk in the warm water. Beat in half the flour, followed by the salt and olive oil. With a wooden spoon, stir in the remaining flour – don't worry about lumpy bits.

Turn out the dough onto a lightly oiled surface and knead (about 20 times) until soft. Replace in the bowl and, with your hands, oil it lightly. Cover with a tea towel and put in a warm place (e.g. a hot press or airing cupboard) for 1½ hours.

Remove the risen dough, knock back the air and knead again (20 times) on an oiled surface. Leave to rise in a warm place for 1½ hours.

Turn out on to the oiled surface again and cut the dough into smaller pieces, about a handful each. Oil a rolling pin and roll out each focaccia, about 10–12.5cm (4–5in) in diameter. Place on baking trays lined with greaseproof paper.

Add your choice of toppings and leave to rise for 1 hour before baking in a preheated oven at 200°C, 400°F, Gas Mark 6 for 20 minutes.

Tip: Alternatively, you can place the focaccia dough in the fridge overnight and then add the toppings the following day and bake as above.

Potato Scones

We've always relied on potatoes in Ireland, often using them as a substitute for flour.

Makes 4
260g (9oz) whole unpeeled potatoes
40g (1¼ oz) butter, plus a little more for frying
salt and freshly ground black pepper
60g (2oz) plain flour

Place the potatoes in a saucepan, cover with water and bring to the boil. Drain off half the liquid and simmer for about 30 minutes (depending on the size of the potatoes) until cooked.

With a tea towel in one hand to hold the hot potato and a peeler in the other, peel the potatoes, then mash with the butter. Leave to cool slightly. Season with salt and pepper, then fold in the flour and mix to form a dough.

Transfer the potato mixture onto a board, then knead lightly and roll out the dough, about 5cm (2in) thick. Cut out circles. Place a knob of butter in a frying pan and cook the potato cakes over a medium heat until golden on each side. Serve hot.

Irish Boxty Pancakes

This is like a tortilla wrap – you can fill the pancakes with cheese and serve with guacamole or salsa (see pages 155 and 159).

Makes 8
160g (5½ oz) plain flour
½ tsp baking powder
400g (14oz) potatoes, peeled and grated
1 egg, beaten
110ml (4fl oz) milk

Sieve the flour and baking powder into a large bowl, then add the grated potatoes and mix. Stir in the beaten egg and milk to form a thick batter.

Place an oiled frying pan over a high heat and pour a dessertspoon of batter into the pan. Cook for 3 minutes on each side, or until golden brown. Serve hot.

Farls

These flat breads are a Northern Irish tradition. This recipe is the perfect solution when you need bread in a hurry, as it can be made quickly and tastes delicious.

Makes 4
400g (14oz) plain white flour
1 tsp bread soda or bicarbonate of soda
180ml (6½ fl oz) water or milk
125ml (4½ fl oz) yogurt
plain flour, for cooking

Mix together the flour and bread soda or bicarbonate of soda in a mixing bowl. Pour in your chosen liquid and the yogurt, mixing with a palette knife (strange, I know, but it works), until you have a soft, dry dough.

You can shape the farls as you please but the traditional way is to form the dough into a ball and then roll it out into a circle just under 1cm (½in) thick and divide into quarters.

Place a heavy-bottomed frying pan over a medium heat and sprinkle lightly with flour. When it starts to brown, place a farl in the pan and cook for 5–6 minutes per side until lightly browned. Remove the farl, sprinkle some more flour into the pan and cook the rest in the same way. Keep in a warm place until you're ready to eat them.

Muriel's Health Loaf

Every time my Aunty Muriel comes to visit she brings her health
loaf and it is usually gone within a couple of hours of her arrival!
The good news is that it is nutritional as well as delicious.

Makes 2 loaves

450g (1lb) wholemeal flour
65g (2¼oz) wheat germ,
    plus extra for dusting
65g (2¼oz) plain white flour
65g (2¼oz) wheat bran
225g (8oz) pin-head oatmeal
2 tsp soft brown sugar
2½ tsp bread soda or
    bicarbonate of soda
1 litre (1¾ pints) buttermilk,
    see tip on page 17

For the topping:

2 tsp (one per loaf)
    wheat germ
2 tsp (one per loaf)
    sesame seeds

Pour all the dry ingredients in to a large bowl and mix together. Then stir in the
buttermilk to make a moist dough.

Divide the dough between 2 greased 900g (2lb) loaf tins which have been dusted
with wheat germ. Smooth the top and make a spacious cross on each one with a
floured knife. Sprinkle with wheat germ and sesame seeds.

Place in a preheated oven at 230°C, 450°F, Gas Mark 8 for 10 minutes, and then
reduce the heat to 140°C, 275°F, Gas Mark 1 and bake for 1 hour.

When the loaves are cooked, remove from the oven and partly cool in the tins,
then turn out and leave to cool completely on a cooling rack.

Rock Buns

Every Saturday morning when I was a child, my mother or older sisters would bake rock buns. The aroma would waft through the whole house; it was better than any alarm clock to get us up and dressed.

Makes 8

220g (8oz) self-raising flour
pinch of salt
110g (4oz) butter, diced
110g (4oz) brown sugar
80g (3oz) currants
15g (½oz) chopped cherries
15g (½oz) chopped candied peel
pinch of nutmeg
1 egg
a little milk

Sieve the flour and salt into a mixing bowl and then rub in the butter. Mix in the sugar, currants, cherries, peel and nutmeg. Beat the egg with a little milk and add to the dry ingredients. Mix with a fork to a stiff mixture.

Grease a baking tray and add rough heaps of the bun mixture. Bake in a preheated oven at 200°C, 400°F, Gas Mark 6 for 15 minutes. Serve warm with Irish butter.

White Country Sourdough

There is something very special about making this distinctively flavoured bread. It is made from a yeast culture grown in a paste of flour and water, known as a 'starter'. Each time the bread is made, a small amount of starter is added to the dough. The original starter can then be 'fed' with more flour and water (see tip). With regular use it can be kept going indefinitely. There is a tradition of passing starters on from one generation to the next.

Makes 1 loaf
For the sourdough starter:
2 tsp dried yeast
300ml (10fl oz) water
240g (8½ oz) strong white flour

For the dough:
1 tsp dried yeast
200ml (7fl oz) water
60g (2oz) rye flour
300g (10oz) strong white flour

First, make the sourdough starter. Sprinkle the dried yeast onto the water and stir until dissolved. Stir in the flour, cover, and leave to ferment for 2 days at room temperature. Stir a couple of times a day.

When the starter is ready, make the dough. Sprinkle the dried yeast onto the water and stir until dissolved. Sieve the flours in to a large bowl and make a well in the centre. Pour in 250ml (9fl oz) of the starter (reserving the rest for a future loaf) and mix in the flour from the sides. Stir in the yeast water until you have a sticky dough.

Turn out the dough on to a lightly floured board and knead until smooth and elastic. Place the dough in a bowl, cover with a tea towel and leave in a warm room to rise for 2 hours.

Knock back (knead) the risen dough, punching out the air, and leave to rest for 15 minutes. Shape into a round loaf, place on a lightly floured baking tray and cover with a tea towel. Leave in a warm room (a hot press or airing cupboard is perfect) for 1½ hours – this is called 'proving'. It allows the bread to rise slowly; the dough should double in size. Bake in a preheated oven at 220°C, 425°F, Gas Mark 7 for 1 hour. When cooked, the loaf should sound hollow when you tap the base. Leave to cool on a cooling rack.

Tip: If you wish to keep your starter going, keep it loosely covered in the fridge. Each time you use it, replenish the remainder with an equal amount of flour and water to that which was removed. No further yeast should be necessary. You will notice a watery liquid film on top of your starter, either mix it back in or drain it off. The starter is a living thing: if it stops raising the bread, it should be discarded and a new starter made.

Fish & Game

Responsible Fishing

Ireland's coast is one of her greatest natural resources. Sandwiched between the Atlantic Ocean and the Irish Sea, her waters have offered up a plentiful supply of fish, shellfish and seaweeds. We have a thriving fishing industry, expert fishmongers and our artisan producers are exporting smoked fish and seaweed-based products around the globe. It all sounds good, and it is. The fish certainly is: it's naturally high in protein, low in bad fats and is a great source of Omega 3 oil. *But,* are we good for the fish?

Over-fishing has left our oceans perilously under-stocked, and fishing methods are seriously damaging the ocean environment. Most nets are not selective, when one species of fish is targeted other species are also hauled in. Greenpeace estimates that globally, a quarter of what is caught is merely killed and discarded.

Fish farming is one solution to decreasing stocks, but fish farms are prone to the same problems as intensive chicken farming. I would urge you to buy organically farmed fish (a halfway house between wild and farmed), which is produced under strict guidelines from the Soil Association and other regulatory bodies. It's reared with regard for its welfare and without artificial additives.

What else can you do? Ninety per cent of fish sold in Ireland goes through the big supermarkets. Yet barely any of them source their fish from sustainable fisheries. Help make the supermarkets accountable by asking why they may sell the least sustainable species (cod, plaice and tuna), and take your custom to local fishmongers and farmers' markets. But do make sure that even your local supplier bought the fish from a sustainable fishery. Seek their advice – tell them you don't want to use cod in a particular recipe, and ask them to recommend an alternative fish.

Finally, eat a variety of fish. We rely too heavily on cod and salmon when the sea around Ireland is full of mackerel and herring. Try my recipe for fried mackerel with chilli and rocket salsa. We have some of the best oyster and mussel beds in the world – eat oysters as fresh as possible with a squeeze of lemon juice, and try steaming mussels with fresh tomatoes and chilli. What about our prawns and fantastic smokehouses? Fish smokes beautifully: try smoked eel or kippers on home-made brown bread with mayonnaise – *mmm,* fantastic!

Clonakilty Market Fish Pie

Opposite my stall at the farmers' market in Clonakilty, West Cork, was a fabulous fresh fish stall run by brothers Sean and Ollie O'Driscoll, who bought fresh fish each morning from the local fishermen at the pier in Schull. Every week I bought a bag of fish from them for a fiver - a special offer they do, and as a result I have made every fish pie under the sun! This is my favourite recipe. I use Hegarty's, an Irish mature Cheddar, as its salty flavour is fabulous with the fish.

Serves 4

500g (1lb 2oz) potatoes, peeled and boiled
7g (¼ oz) butter
salt and freshly ground black pepper
4 fillets ling, whiting, or any white fish you can
    get your hands on (approx. 600g/1lb 5oz)
125ml (4½fl oz) milk
50g (2oz) Cheddar cheese, grated
    (e.g. Hegarty's Cheddar)
1 tsp fresh thyme leaves
1 tsp Dijon mustard
50g (2oz) fresh breadcrumbs

Mash the boiled potatoes with a knob of butter and season to taste with salt and black pepper.

Grease an ovenproof dish with the remaining butter and arrange the fish fillets in the base. Season with salt and pepper and pour in the milk.

In a small bowl, mix the grated cheese, thyme and mustard, and spread on top of the fish. Add the remaining mashed potatoes, and sprinkle the fresh breadcrumbs over the top.

Bake in a preheated oven at 200°C, 400°F, Gas Mark 6 for 20 minutes. Serve with green beans, ratatouille (see page 110) or a simple green salad.

Hot Buttered Prawns on Toast

This is one of my favourite recipes – it makes a fabulous light supper or a very decadent starter.

Serves 2
butter, for frying and for toast
12 raw king prawns, shelled
juice of 1 lemon
freshly ground black pepper
4 slices good-quality bread

Place a frying pan over a high heat and add a big knob of butter. When the butter has melted, throw in the prawns and squeeze in all the lemon juice with a good sprinkling of black pepper.

Toast the bread, butter it and pile the prawns on top (3 prawns per slice). Drizzle all the pan juices over them and enjoy. Heaven!

The Irish Farmers' Market Cookbook

Fried Mackerel with Chilli and Rocket Salsa

At one of the first Slow Food markets I organised in Baltimore, a fishing village in West Cork, I asked Frank Hederman (a fish smoker, see following pages) to bring me a big bag of fresh mackerel, and a big bag he did bring – 200 fish in total! I set up a grill and spent the day cooking this delicious recipe. It was fantastic to see kids, fishermen, mums and dads and even very cool teenagers scoffing down their mackerel. It's a wonderful fish.

Serves 2
knob of butter
2 fresh mackerel, filleted
salt and freshly ground
    black pepper
1 lemon, optional

For the salsa:
1 small bunch of rocket,
    finely chopped
1 red tiger chilli,
      deseeded and finely
      chopped
juice of 1 lemon

First make the chilli and rocket salsa by placing all ingredients in a bowl and mixing well.

Place a frying pan over a high heat, melt in the butter and cook the fish, skin side down, for 2 minutes (adding a sprinkling of salt and pepper). Turn the fish over and cook for a further 2 minutes.

Place the cooked mackerel on a warm plate and accompany with the chilli and rocket salsa and a wedge of lemon. Serve immediately.

Frank Hederman from Belvelly Smokehouse

Belvelly Smokehouse is the oldest smokehouse in Ireland. Run by Frank Hederman, Belvelly is best known for its smoked wild Irish salmon, prized for the subtle flavours characterised by a unique balance in taste between the fish and the beechwood smoke. All the fish are wild and sourced locally, or have been cultivated to organic certification. When wild salmon is in short supply, Frank uses Glenarm salmon, an organic fish that is reared off the coast of County Antrim, where the strong tides ensure a good lean texture and a beautiful smoked product.

Frank with his delicious smoked mackerel.

Frank is a passionate advocate for the highest standards and quality in artisan food production. At the smokehouse he uses only the finest ingredients to craft his end product, which include smoked mussels, mackerel, eel and haddock, as well as his award-winning salmon.

Frank started out in the early eighties alongside many of the early cheese makers and other artisan food producers. His motivation for going into salmon smoking wasn't passion (that came later), but an eye for a good business opportunity. He grew up in Cobh where there was a strong fishing - and fish processing - culture and he needed to make a living. Like the farmers who turned their surplus of milk into cheese, Frank saw smoking as a good way to add value to salmon and other fish.

In 1996 he started trading at his first outdoor market, the Coal Quay Market - now known as Cornmarket - although locals still call it Coal Quay. A year later he was one of the pioneers at Temple Bar (a market in central Dublin). In at the beginning of the food revolution with a great product, Frank soon had stalls in Holywood, Co. Down, and eventually at other markets around Co. Dublin. The English market was a natural progression as he developed retail outlets and grew the business. He took a stall when Midleton Market started in 2000 and still sells there, as well as at Mahon Point and Cobh. When I first started at Midleton Market, I didn't have the cash to invest in a proper umbrella and stall, but Frank bought them for me without question and allowed me to pay him back when my stall got busier. It taught me that farmers' markets aren't just about making money but that they are also about camaraderie

Frank's stall selling smoked fish and patés.

and community – may this ethos stay alive. I would like to take this opportunity to say thank you to Frank for his unquestioning support throughout my days at the markets.

Belvelly is always looking for ways to develop new products. Recently they have produced smoked mussels marinated in vinaigrette, which are delicious just as they are, great in salads or on hot buttered brown toast canapés. The marinated mussels are also sold in pure olive oil, so that they can be used in hot dishes too. I think they are a fantastic idea for all cooks looking for that little extra inspiration. Rich and flavoursome, just two to four per person would flavour chowder, a risotto, or a leek tart.

Frank's Smoked Eel with Celeriac and Crème Fraîche

It has been said by many renowned food writers that Frank Hederman (see previous pages) does the best smoked eel in the world – and I agree.

Serves 4
1 small celeriac
200ml (7fl oz) crème fraîche
50g (2oz) whole hazelnuts
salt and freshly ground
    black pepper
butter
8 brown bread slices
20cm (8in) piece smoked eel

Peel and grate the celeriac. Blanch by placing in a saucepan of boiling water for 2 minutes, then drain well. Fold the celeriac through the crème fraîche.

Roast the hazelnuts in a preheated oven at 200°C, 400°F, Gas Mark 6 for 10 minutes. Leave them to cool slightly before chopping finely and folding through the crème fraîche and celeriac. Season to taste with salt and pepper.

Butter the brown bread, lay the smoked eel on top and add a spoonful of the creamed celeriac.

Summer Fish Stew

I throw in the rice so I don't have to worry about providing side dishes, but if you don't like rice, just omit it and serve the dish with piping hot boiled potatoes.

Serves 4

800g (1lb 10oz) white fish (e.g. ling, pollock, etc., including bones and heads), filleted and cut into small chunks

1.7 litres (3 pints) water

2 black peppercorns

1 bay leaf

1 carrot, sliced

1 onion, sliced

2 tbsp olive oil

2 garlic cloves

1 onion, finely chopped

2.5cm (1in) fresh root ginger, peeled and crushed

250ml (9 fl oz) white wine

400g (14oz) passata (sieved tomatoes)

1 tsp turmeric

1 tsp paprika

10 black olives, stoned and chopped

8 cherry tomatoes, halved

225g (8oz) rice

juice of 1 lime

salt and freshly ground black pepper

bunch of fresh basil, torn

First, make the fish stock. Place the fish bones and heads in a large saucepan and cover with the water. Throw in the peppercorns, bay leaf, sliced carrot and onion. Bring to the boil and leave to simmer, uncovered, for 30–40 minutes. Strain well.

Place a heavy-bottomed saucepan over a medium heat, pour in the olive oil, and then add the garlic, chopped onion and ginger. Cover and sweat for 2 minutes. Remove the lid and add the white wine, passata, turmeric, paprika, olives, cherry tomatoes, 150ml (5fl oz) of the fish stock and the rice. Leave to cook for 10 minutes. Add the fish and cook for a further 5 minutes until cooked through.

Squeeze in the lime juice, season with salt and pepper and stir in the fresh basil leaves. Serve in bowls with some white chunky bread on the side to soak up all the delicious juices!

Tip: Making fresh fish stock makes a huge difference to the overall taste of the stew and it uses up all the bones that would ordinarily be thrown out. It is preferable to use white fish, rather than oily varieties, which can be pungent and gelatinous. If you don't have the time to make fish stock ask at your local good food store which is the best brand of fish stock to buy.

Pan-fried Black Sole with Wild Garlic Butter

Wild garlic is in season in spring. The leaves are delicious to cook with and the edible flowers are fantastic for decorating the plate.

Serves 2
4 fillets of black sole
wild garlic flowers
salt and freshly ground
  black pepper

For the wild garlic butter:
110g (4oz) butter, softened
1 small bunch of wild garlic
  leaves, chopped

First, make the garlic butter. Ensure that the butter has been kept out of the fridge at room temperature for about 2 hours – it should be nice and soft. Place the butter and wild garlic leaves in a bowl and cream together with the back of a spoon.

Heat a frying pan and melt one-third of the garlic butter. Add the sole fillets and cook for about 4 minutes until golden. Season with salt and pepper. Reduce the heat to medium and cook the sole fillets for 4 minutes on the other side. Remove to warm serving plates.

Add the remaining wild garlic butter to the pan and when it has melted drizzle over the fillets. Garnish with the wild garlic flowers and enjoy!

Goujons of Plaice with Sweet Chilli Sauce

I have used plaice in this recipe as the delicate fish makes a delicious contrast to the crispy crunch of the batter. However, you can use virtually any fish.

Serves 2
500g (1lb 2oz) plaice, filleted
150g (5oz) plain flour
2 tbsp sesame seeds
salt and freshly ground
    black pepper
sunflower oil, for frying
600ml (1 pint) fresh milk
1 lemon, quartered

For the sweet chilli sauce:
1 fresh red chilli, finely
    chopped
1 tbsp soy sauce
1 tbsp sesame oil
1 tsp honey

Cut the fillets of plaice into strips. Tip the flour and sesame seeds into a large bowl, season with salt and pepper and mix well.

Pour the oil into a deep frying pan (the oil should be about 5cm [2in] deep) and place over a high heat. When the oil begins to smoke, reduce the heat to medium. Dip the pieces of fish into the milk and then into the flour mixture. Drop them into the hot oil and fry until crisp and golden then turn and repeat.

Mix together the ingredients for the sweet chilli sauce and serve with the crisply fried plaice fillets and a wedge of lemon.

Fish Cakes with Tzatziki

I make these fish cakes nice and thin, like biscuits, because it makes them lighter and the taste more intense – and they look beautiful.

Serves 4

200g (7oz) fish (e.g. perch, ling, or haddock)
600ml (1 pint) milk
2 black peppercorns
200g (7oz) mashed potato
250ml (9 fl oz) olive oil, for frying
1 red pepper, deseeded and finely chopped
2 spring onions (scallions), finely chopped
juice of ½ lemon
salt and freshly ground black pepper
1 egg yolk
flour, for coating
fresh coriander leaves, to garnish
tzatziki, to serve (see page 71)

Poach the fish by placing it in a saucepan and covering with milk. Add the black peppercorns and cook gently over a medium heat for about 15 minutes. Cooking times will vary according to the fish, so break some up with a spoon to check that it is cooked right through.

Drain and place the fish in a large bowl with the mashed potato. Pull up your sleeves, wash your hands and mix the fish and potato together with your hands.

Place a frying pan over a medium heat and pour in a drop of olive oil. Add the red pepper and spring onions and cook until soft.

Stir the cooked pepper and spring onions into the fish and potato mixture, then add the lemon juice and season well with salt and pepper. Bind together with the egg yolk, and then divide the mixture into 8 little balls. Flatten them out with your hands (don't be too concerned about them being the same size – it's home cooking, after all!). Dip the fish cakes into a bowl of seasoned flour and flip them back and forth in your hands to shake off any excess flour.

Put the frying pan back on the heat, add a splash of olive oil and fry the fish cakes, turning when they are golden brown beneath. This should take about 4 minutes per side as they are quite thin. Serve warm with tzatziki, garnished with coriander leaves.

Steamed Mussels with Tomato, Chilli and Garlic

I get a bag of fresh mussels about every two weeks at the English Market in Cork City. This is such a simple and delicious dish to cook when you have lots of people coming for dinner.

Serves 2

400g (14oz) live mussels, scrubbed
2 tbsp olive oil
3 garlic cloves, crushed
2 chillies, deseeded and finely chopped
400g (14oz) tomatoes, chopped
250ml (9 fl oz) white wine
salt and freshly ground black pepper
2 spring onions (scallions), sliced
1 bunch of fresh coriander, coarsely chopped
juice of 1 lemon

How do I clean and prepare mussels?

First, check if the mussels are alive (dead ones should be discarded). To do this place them under cold running water, if they close they're good to eat, if they remain open throw them away.

Clean the shells by placing them under cold running water and scrub off any dirt. Pull the beard off the closed shells

Place a heavy-bottomed saucepan over a medium heat and add the olive oil. When the oil is hot, add the garlic and chillies and cook gently for 2 minutes. Add the chopped tomatoes and white wine, cover the pan and cook for a further 5 minutes.

Season with salt and pepper, and then add the cleaned mussels and spring onions. Cover the pan and cook over a medium heat until all the mussels have opened – this should take about 8–10 minutes, shaking the pan gently and tossing them in the tomatoes every couple of minutes. (Throw away any mussels that do not open after cooking.)

Scatter the coriander over the mussels and pour the lemon juice over the top just before serving. Eat with a big basket of sourdough (see page 27) to soak up all the juices!

Seafood Risotto

For centuries, seaweed has been part of the Irish diet, which is not really surprising as we have a coastline of over 3,000km (1,864 miles). It is renewable, plentiful and packed with nutrients, potassium and iodine. It sustained communities throughout the famine and is still eaten in pubs in the north, dried and fried, as an alternative to crisps. Smoked dilisk adds a subtle flavour to this risotto, and is widely available in health food stores and fishmongers (see Directory for suppliers).

Serves 6

2 tbsp olive oil
1 medium onion, diced
1 red pepper, deseeded and diced
2 garlic cloves, crushed
500g (1lb 2oz) risotto rice
salt and freshly ground black pepper
500ml (17½ fl oz) hot fish stock
100ml (3½ fl oz) dry white wine
300g (10oz) white fish (e.g. cod,
    haddock or ling), cut into 2.5cm
    (1in) pieces

5g (1/6oz) smoked dilisk
500g (1lb 2oz) fresh, cleaned mussels
    (see page 44 for guidelines)
500g (1lb 2oz) langoustines, whole
    in their shells
50g (2oz) Desmond cheese
    (or Parmesan)
lemon wedges, to serve

Place a saucepan over a medium heat, drizzle in the olive oil and add the onion, pepper and garlic. Cover and cook for 15 minutes, stirring occasionally.

Stir the rice into the pan and season with salt and pepper. Slowly add in the hot fish stock and white wine, stirring as you do, then add in the white fish and smoked dilisk. Continue to cook until the rice has absorbed all the liquid, stirring often. When the rice is al dente (still a bit of a bite) stir in the cleaned mussels and langoustines. Cover and leave to simmer for a further 10 minutes or until the mussels have opened.

Grate some Desmond (or Parmesan) cheese over the top, and serve hot with lemon wedges.

Olivier and Maja

Olivier Beajouan and his partner, Maja Binder, are a marriage made in gastro heaven! They live and work in Castlegregory, overlooking the Atlantic, in a commercial kitchen, smokehouse and dairy, which was built and renovated entirely themselves. Maja produces Dingle Peninsula cheese and Olivier makes Irish seaweed-based products. Their separate passions come together in Maja's cheese, which is flavoured with Olivier's seaweed.

Olivier came to sea vegetables through a course he was taking in shiatsu. As part of the course he studied nutrition and foraged for wild food in the forest and sea. He became fascinated by the possibilities of seaweed and of reviving the seaweed food culture. He started out making seaweed pâté, but as his success has grown he has expanded his product base to include a sensational tapenade of sea vegetables, pickled kombu, and my favourite: spaghetti-shaped seaweed marinated in fresh ginger, tomato and vinegar. It is wonderful with fresh taglioni, a drizzle of olive oil and grated Desmond cheese. Olivier also produces fantastic fish sausages with lemon, spices, seaweed and onion. They taste great and are very low in fat.

Traditionally, seaweed was washed, cut into strips and cooked with boiled potatoes and bacon, or used in soups and stews as a thickener. It sustained communities throughout the famine, but people stopped eating it regularly when other vegetables became more readily available. Today, thanks to producers like Olivier, seaweed is enjoying a renaissance as a vegetable in its own right.

Maja made cheese in Italy, the Swiss Alps and Germany before coming to Ireland to produce hard and semi-hard cow's milk cheeses. Maja follows the ancient Irish tradition of flavouring cheese with seaweed. Her gold award-winning Dilisk cheese is flavoured with dark red sea grass, which speckles the cheese's pale yellow hue and adds a hint of salt.

Maja uses raw cows' milk, all from one herd, to make the cheese. Like all the great cheese producers, she believes you cannot get the individual flavours that make a cheese unique to a particular place if you don't use unpasteurised milk. When she first started selling the cheese, customers were unaccustomed, and a little scared, by the mould that grows on the outside of the cheese. However, the cheese tasted so good they kept coming back. Next time you're at the farmers' markets look out for raw-milk cheeses and seaweed products.

Maja and Olivier with all their fantastic cheeses.

Seared Scallops with a Madeira Dressing on Rocket

Terry Sherran, chef at Mackerel in Dublin, cooked this dish for me. It is the most delicious way I have ever eaten scallops – the tastes are so beautifully delicate.

Serves 2

240ml (8¼fl oz) dry sherry
350ml (12 fl oz) Madeira
25g (1oz) brown sugar
1 shallot, diced
5 star anise
1 sprig fresh thyme
60ml (2fl oz) sesame oil
60ml (2fl oz) soy sauce
60ml (2fl oz) truffle oil, or
    a very good olive oil
6-8 large scallops, or 10-12
    small ones
1 tbsp olive oil
salt and freshly ground
    black pepper
1 large bunch of rocket

Put the sherry, Madeira, brown sugar, diced shallot, star anise and thyme in a saucepan over a high heat and cook until reduced in volume by two-thirds. Leave to cool and then strain through a sieve. Whisk in the sesame oil, soy sauce and truffle oil.

To cook the scallops, place a frying pan over a high heat and add the olive oil. Season the scallops on both sides and cook for 2 minutes each side.

Dress the rocket leaves with a little of the Madeira dressing and arrange on serving plates. Place the scallops on top and drizzle over the remaining dressing. Eat straight away!

Tip: Always buy fresh, organic scallops. They should be cooked very quickly over a high heat and are better slightly undercooked rather than overcooked.

Wild food

I think game isn't something many of us know a great deal about. We probably think it's something men in flat caps and plus fours with red noses and double-barrel shotguns go hunting for at certain times of the year. We don't really know where to buy it, how to cook it and to be honest don't really go a bundle on the taste. Well, I think it's worth a second chance.

So, when is the gaming season? It kicks off in mid-August and draws to a close around the end of January. It is called 'game' in reference to the sport of shooting, but 'gamey' has come to describe the rich, intense flavour we associate with eating wild meat. Game that can be found at the Irish markets include: deer, pheasant, duck, grouse, snipe, woodcock, goose, rabbit and hare.

The taste is a result of the animal's diet, the fact that the muscle is lean, and the way the meat is hung. Hanging relaxes the meat, making it more tender and intensifying the flavour. The amount of time an animal is hung depends on its size and the temperature of the room.

So why are we reluctant to eat game? I think there is a lack of knowledge about how it is prepared. You can ask your butcher to prepare the meat for you and discuss how long it has been hung. There is also a confusion about how to cook game – the lean meat can dry out very quickly. There are, however, many ways round this: cook it with pork belly or a fatty meat; cook it in large chunks if you are making stew; and, in the case of venison, cook it quickly on a high heat, or if you are cooking a joint, cover it in bacon rashers. Look out for game the next time you visit your local farmers' market or butcher and give this wonderful meat a try.

The Irish Farmers' Market Cookbook

Chocolate and Venison Stew

This may seem an unusual combination but there is a rich tradition of using chocolate in savoury dishes. I first tasted the marriage of chocolate and venison at a Slow Food market in Kenmare, where the legendary chef, Dave Gumbelton, had a stall with Enrico Fantastia (a Venetian wine merchant and also a great chef). Dave had a huge pot of this stew, and the flavour was incredible!

Dave was one of the most passionate and talented chefs. Sadly, he passed away in 2004, but his passion, kindness and glorious food will be remembered forever by anyone who ever had the pleasure of meeting him.

Serves 4

2 tbsp olive oil	3 tbsp unsweetened cocoa powder
100g (3½ oz) smoked streaky bacon or pancetta, diced	1 tbsp smoked paprika
	6 garlic cloves, crushed
150g (5oz) shallots, left whole	250ml (9 fl oz) red wine
500g (1lb 2oz) diced venison or venison shin	750ml (24 fl oz) chicken or beef stock
	salt and freshly ground black pepper

Place a casserole dish over a medium heat and add the olive oil. When the oil begins to smoke, add the bacon or pancetta and cook until golden. Then add the shallots and leave to caramelise. Remove the shallots and bacon or pancetta from the casserole and set aside.

Add the venison and brown on all sides over a high heat, then stir in the cocoa powder, paprika and garlic. Cook for 1–2 minutes, remove and then deglaze the dish by adding the red wine to the casserole dish over a high heat and stirring all the juices and food bites into the wine. Cook until reduced to two-thirds of its original volume and then add all the ingredients back to the casserole dish.

Pour the stock into the casserole and bring to a simmer. Then cover the casserole with a lid and bake in a preheated oven at 150°C, 300°F, Gas Mark 2 for 1–1½ hours. Check the seasoning and serve hot with whipped potato or even just some good-quality bread.

The Irish Farmers' Market Cookbook

Rabbit Stew with Cider

The sweetness in the cider and honey is fantastic with the rabbit. This dish is great served with rice or pandy.

Serves 4

2 tbsp olive oil	4 garlic cloves, crushed
300g (10 oz) streaky bacon, chopped	2 tbsp honey
	1 sprig fresh thyme
1 wild rabbit, skinned and jointed	1 bay leaf
	400ml (14 fl oz) cider
12 baby carrots	salt and freshly ground
8 shallots, peeled and whole	black pepper

Heat a frying pan and add the olive oil. Add the bacon and sauté until golden and crisp. Remove the bacon to a casserole dish.

Add the rabbit joints to the frying pan, sauté until golden and then place in the casserole dish.

Lastly, add the carrots, shallots, garlic and honey to the pan and cook until caramelised. Transfer to the casserole dish, season with salt and pepper and pop in the thyme and bay leaf. Cover with the cider.

Cook in a preheated oven at 120°C, 250°F, Gas Mark ½ for 2 hours. Serve with pandy (see page 96).

Venison Terrine

Eat this terrine with a fruity chutney and some warm chunky bread. It's great for picnics, lunch or as a starter.

'Forcemeat' is a paste made from meat, poultry or game and then mixed with fruit, nuts or breadcrumbs. It is used as a stuffing and as a binding agent in pâtés and terrines.

Makes 1 loaf

900g (2lb) venison meat (from the leg or fillet), cut into pieces
2 tbsp sunflower oil
400g (14oz) streaky bacon rashers, stretched out thin with the back of a knife

For the forcemeat:

500g (1lb 2oz) sausage meat
200g (7oz) chicken livers, chopped
1 tbsp chopped fresh thyme
50g (2oz) pistachios, shelled
2 garlic cloves, crushed
3 tbsp brandy
1 egg, beaten
salt and freshly ground black pepper

Firstly, make the forcemeat by putting the sausage meat, chicken livers, thyme, pistachios, crushed garlic cloves, brandy and beaten egg in a large bowl. Then season with salt and pepper and mix well. Set aside.

Place a frying pan over a medium heat, add a splash of sunflower oil. Cut the venison into strips and add to the pan. Cook until brown all over.

Line a 900g (2lb) loaf tin with the stretched streaky bacon rashers and make sure to overlap the edges of the rashers. You'll need to have enough bacon to fold over the top of the terrine once it is filled. Spread a layer (about one-third) of the forcemeat in the base of the lined tin, and then add a layer of venison. Continue layering up the terrine in this way, seasoning lightly between the layers and finishing with a layer of forcemeat.

Fold the strips of bacon overhanging the dish over the top and cover with a sheet of kitchen foil. Stand in a bain-marie, or stand in a roasting pan half filled with water. Bake in a preheated oven at 180°C, 350°F, Gas Mark 4 for 1½ hours.

Leave to cool completely in a cool place and press down with a board and a 900g (2lb) weight until cold. This compacts the layers, allowing the terrine to cut easily.

Roast Pheasant with Apple and Sweet Geranium Sauce

The most important thing to remember when cooking pheasant is not to overcook it as it dries out easily, so make sure that you smear the bird with plenty of butter before roasting.

Serves 2

25g (1 oz) butter
1 pheasant (approx.
    700g/1lb 9oz)
salt and freshly ground black
    pepper
1 cooking apple, peeled,
    cored and roughly
    chopped

**For the apple and
sweet geranium sauce:**

500g (1lb 2oz) cooking apples, peeled,
    cored and chopped
2 tsp water
50g (2 oz) sugar
4 sweet geranium leaves (see tip page 200)

Rub some butter around the cavity of the pheasant, season with salt and pepper, and then place the apple inside. Smear the remaining butter over the outside of the bird and season with salt and pepper.

Place in a roasting pan and cook in a preheated oven at 190°C, 375°F, Gas Mark 5 for 55–60 minutes. Use the pan juices to make a gravy, if wished.

While the pheasant is roasting, make the sauce. Place the apples in a saucepan with the water, sugar and geranium leaves. Cover and leave to simmer gently until the apple has turned to mush. Remove the leaves. Whisk gently and serve warm with the pheasant.

Tip: Game Chips are so delicious and quite simple to make. They are traditionally eaten during the game season when vegetables such as potatoes, parsnips, turnips and beetroot are available. You can use any of these, simply slice the vegetable of your choice very thinly using a mandolin or sharp knife and cook in a hot deep fat fryer using vegetable oil. Drain the slices using kitchen paper and sprinkle with sea salt.

Meat & Poultry

Meaty Issues

Buying meat today raises bigger issues than simply how well-done you like your beef. The many different labels on the packaging pander to our various concerns about meat: the quality, where it came from, the welfare of the animals. In fact, many of those labels hide more than they reveal. I always advocate that you buy locally and that you buy from your butcher rather than the supermarket. Why? Well, I don't like buying food from someone who has no contact with the producer, who can't tell me where it came from and probably doesn't know the best way to cook it.

Provenance is important. It matters to me that the meat is from local farms and that the butcher can tell me what kind of cattle they raise, what the cattle are fed on and how they are reared. Because the meat I buy is sourced locally it is fresher, and fewer food miles are used getting it from the field onto my plate. I get peace of mind knowing where the meat has come from – I don't have to worry that it travelled thousands of miles, frozen in the tank of a container ship.

Quality is important, but how do we recognise it? Put simply, intensively reared cattle are bred for high yield and accelerated growth. They are often raised in confined indoor spaces, fed cocktails of drugs to stop disease spreading and are given growth hormones so that they reach maturity quicker. The result is pale, weepy meat with little taste and that dries out in the oven because it has no fat to keep it moist. By contrast good meat should be a darker red; because the cattle have been raised outdoors slowly the meat will have fat on it, ensuring flavour, texture and moisture during cooking.

Next time you're in a supermarket try asking one of the assistants how long the meat was hung. Supermarkets don't hang meat because it takes time and space, and because the carcass loses moisture during hanging, which means less weight, which means less profit. High-quality meat, however, will have been hung and will be dry – almost sticky to touch.

Perhaps I pay a little more in my local butcher's than I would in a supermarket, but for that I get knowledge, skill, service and much better quality meat. I value the relationship I have with my butcher. I learn from his expertise; I benefit from his skill; he'll recommend a good cut of meat or suggest a particular recipe and he welcomes feedback. I trust him. I know where his meat has come from, I know it hasn't been pumped full of hormones and additives and hosed down with water to increase the weight. I can request the cut of meat I want; I can place special orders: a goose for Christmas, or a woodcock for a special dinner party. In a supermarket I don't 'choose' my meat - I take what I am given. At the butchers, I can ask for the size cubes I want cut when I'm making stew and I can ask him to leave on a little of the fat for flavour.

Supermarkets have decided that fat is unfashionable so I can't pick up a beautiful cut of marbled beef (threads of fat that run through the meat), which give a dish fantastic flavour.

By buying locally produced, organic or free-range meat from the butcher you are making a choice. You are choosing to deal with farmers who protect the welfare of their livestock. You are choosing quality over cost – buying meat that has real nutritional value and real taste. By taking this simple step you are directly helping to change the system.

Malahide Market Steak Sandwich with Caramelised Onions

I cooked this sandwich for customers at the wonderful Malahide farmers' market outside Dublin. The caramelised onions and red peppers are so good with the fillet steaks, for me this is true 'fast food'!

Serves 2

4 tbsp olive oil
1 medium onion, thinly
    sliced
1 medium red pepper,
    deseeded and sliced

2 tbsp brown sugar or honey
2 x 115g (4oz) fillet steaks
4 slices chunky white bread
    (sourdough if you can get
    it, or see page 27)
handful of fresh rocket
salt and freshly ground
    black pepper

Place a heavy-bottomed saucepan over a low heat and add 2 tablespoons olive oil. When the oil is hot, add the onion and red pepper, cover the pan and leave to simmer until soft. When softened, stir in the sugar or honey, turn up the heat and cook, uncovered, mixing with a spoon every couple of minutes, until they begin to caramelise.

Meanwhile, heat 1 tablespoon olive oil in a frying pan and add the steaks. Fry for 3–4 minutes each side, depending on how you like them cooked, and season with salt and pepper.

Place the bread on a griddle pan and grill until toasted. Remove the bread from the griddle and place on a plate. Cover each slice with lots of fresh rocket and a drizzle of olive oil. Slice the steaks thinly and divide between the sandwiches. Top with the caramelised onions and peppers and serve immediately.

Barrie Tyner's Home-made Beef Burger

My cousin, Barrie Tyner, has a stall called The West Cork Deli at Midleton and Ennis farmers' markets, where he cooks free-range meats, then wraps them in delicious freshly baked breads topped with home-made relishes.

Makes 4 burgers

900g (2lb) good-quality beef, coarsely ground
1 onion, diced
2 tsp chopped fresh thyme
salt and freshly ground
black pepper
1 egg yolk, beaten
50ml (2 fl oz) olive oil
4 burger buns or 8 slices of bread
summer cucumber pickle to serve (see page 177)

Place the beef in a large bowl and mix in the onion, thyme and seasoning. Bind the mixture together with the egg yolk. Shape into 4 burgers with your hands.

Get your frying pan or griddle pan nice and hot and add a splash of oil, then place the burgers on the pan or grill and cook for 4 minutes each side.

Serve on toasted buns with the cucumber pickle (or your favourite condiment).

Cork Beef Stew

As part of their celebration of Irish food in 2004, Selfridges asked superb vegetarian chef, Denis Cotter of Café Paradiso in Cork, and me to design their 'ready-to-go food' counter. This was by far the most popular dish I created. It is slow-cooked for a long time, so the beef becomes really tender and absorbs all the flavours of the bacon, mushrooms and the stout, which works so well in beef stews. I suggest you serve it with mashed potato (pandy) but it is equally good with rice or chunky bread and butter to mop up the juices.

Serves 8

25g (1oz) dripping
150g (5oz) bacon lardons
300g (10oz) shallots, peeled
    and left whole
1kg (2lb 4oz) stewing beef,
    cubed
salt and freshly ground
    black pepper
400g (14oz) mixed wild
    mushrooms
1 litre (1³/₄ pints) stout,
    such as Murphy's
1 bouquet garni

Melt the dripping in a hot frying pan and add the bacon, then the shallots. Cook until golden brown and transfer to a large casserole.

Add the beef to the frying pan, season with salt and pepper and cook until browned all over. Transfer to the casserole.

Lastly, add the mushrooms to the pan and cook for 2 minutes then season and transfer to the casserole.

Place the frying pan back over the heat and using a whisk scrape off all the bits stuck to the bottom of the pan (this is where the flavour is!). Pour in the stout and continue to whisk for another minute; this process is called deglazing. Then pour the stout and pan juices over the beef and vegetables in the casserole. Add the bouquet garni, cover the casserole and cook in a preheated oven at 140°C, 275°F, Gas Mark 1 for 2 hours. Check the seasoning, take out the bouquet garni and serve with pandy (see page 96).

O'Flynn's Rib of Beef with Creamy Black Pepper and Rosemary Gravy

I get all my beef from Simon and Patrick O'Flynn in Cork city. Their father, John, started selling meat in The Old English Market in 1927 and Simon took over in the 1950s. They moved from the market in 1980 to their premises on Marlboro Street, where they have built up a reputation as one of the best butchers in Ireland.

Serves 4

1.5–2kg (2½–5lb) rib of beef on the bone (see tip)	1 tsp sea salt
	1 tbsp cracked black pepper
4 sprigs fresh rosemary	600ml (1 pint) single cream
4 garlic cloves, peeled	

Preparing the joint for roasting could not be simpler: With a sharp knife, make 4 holes in the top side of the rib of beef and push a sprig of rosemary and a clove of garlic into each hole. Rub the sea salt and 1 teaspoon cracked pepper into the meat. Place the meat, bone-side down, on a rack in a shallow roasting pan. Before putting the meat into the oven allow it to reach room temperature – if it's cold from the fridge it will affect your cooking times.

Put the beef, uncovered, into a preheated hot oven at 220°C, 425°F, Gas Mark 7 for 30 minutes until browned. Once browned continue cooking for 9–10 minutes per 500g (1lb 2oz) for rare beef; 12–15 minutes for medium; and 18–20 minutes if you like your beef well done.

Remove the cooked joint from oven, cover it with a foil tent and leave to stand for 30 minutes. This allows the juices to retreat and the meat will be more tender once rested. It also gives you time to deglaze the roasting pan for the gravy.

Place the roasting pan over a low heat and pour in the cream and the remaining cracked pepper. With a whisk, gather all the delicious juices from the beef and mix it with the cream. The creamy gravy will begin to thicken after a couple of minutes. Serve the gravy hot with the beef.

Tip: I recommend you buy a rib of beef on the bone, not only because it improves the taste but the bone also creates a standing rack, which makes carving easier. Buy a rib with some fat on it – this will give it moisture and flavour.

The Best Shepherd's Pie

My great friend Regina Sexton (an Irish food historian and author of *A Little History of Irish Food*) and I one day set ourselves a challenge of coming up with the best shepherd's pie recipe ever, and here it is...

Serves 6

2 tbsp olive oil
1 onion, diced
1½ carrots, diced
700g (1lb 9oz) minced lamb
3 tsp tomato purée
1 tsp Dijon mustard
250ml (9 fl oz) hot stock
(beef or chicken)

salt and freshly ground black
pepper
creamy mashed potato
(pandy, see page 96),
allow approx. 200g (7oz)
per person
2 tbsp melted butter

Place a flameproof casserole dish over a medium heat and add the olive oil. When the oil is hot, add the onion and carrots, then cover and reduce the heat so that they sweat.

When they are nicely softened, remove the lid and turn up the heat to high. Add the minced lamb and cook until brown. Stir in the tomato purée and mustard, and then add the hot stock. Season with salt and pepper and simmer over a low heat for 15 minutes.

Cover the mixture with the creamy mashed potato and brush the top with melted butter to get a crispy golden finish. Cook in a preheated oven at 180°C, 350°F, Gas Mark 4 for 50 minutes.

Slow-roasted Lamb Shanks with Fresh Ginger, Apricots, Tomatoes and Couscous

When lamb shanks are slow roasted they become so tender that the meat just tumbles off the bone when you touch it with your fork. The dried fruits, spices, tomatoes and crunchy almonds add great flavour. This classic Moroccan-style dish is definitely one of my favourite comfort foods.

Serves 2

3 tbsp olive oil

1 tbsp cumin seeds

1 onion, finely chopped

4 medium sweet potatoes, peeled and diced

2 garlic cloves, crushed

2 medium-sized lamb shanks

400g (14oz) can chopped tomatoes

300g (10oz) dried apricots, roughly chopped

salt and black pepper

2 tbsp flaked almonds

375g (13oz) couscous

500ml (17½ fl oz) boiling water or chicken stock (see page 126)

few sprigs fresh coriander, torn

Heat 1 tablespoon olive oil in a casserole or heavy-bottomed saucepan over a medium heat. Add the cumin seeds and toast for 2 minutes. Stir in the onion, sweet potatoes and garlic, cover the pan and simmer for 5 minutes.

Add the lamb shanks, browning them on each side. Add the tomatoes and apricots, and season. Cover the pan and leave to simmer for 2 hours.

Heat a frying pan over a low heat and add the almonds, tossing all the time as they burn quite easily - you are aiming for a light brown shade.

Place the couscous in a large bowl and pour over the boiling water (or chicken stock). Place a plate on top of the bowl to act as a lid and leave the couscous to steam for 10 minutes. When all the liquid has been absorbed, add the remaining olive oil and break up the grains with a fork. Fold in the almonds.

Divide the couscous between 2 plates and place a lamb shank in its sauce on top. Sprinkle with coriander and serve.

Mum's Irish Stew

I reckon everyone in Ireland counts their mum's Irish stew as the best they ever tasted. That's what so great about the food you grow up with – it conjures up feelings of being cared for. This recipe is simple and traditional, but you can vary and embellish it in lots of ways. Try adding smoked bacon lardons, pearl barley or turnips. When buying the stewing lamb from your butcher, don't forget to ask for a lamb bone for the stock – stock cubes don't taste as good.

Serves 4-6
15g (1/2 oz) butter
4 carrots, diced
salt and freshly ground
    black pepper
4 medium onions, finely chopped
6 waxy, medium potatoes, peeled
    and cut into large chunks
900g (2lb) stewing lamb, cut
    into chunks
2 sprigs fresh thyme

For the stock:
1 lamb bone
1 carrot
1 onion
2 peppercorns
1 bouquet garni

First, make the stock. Place all the ingredients in a saucepan and fill with cold water. Bring to the boil and simmer for as long as possible to bring out the flavour; 2–3 hours, if you can.

Place a flameproof casserole dish over a high heat and melt the butter. Throw in the carrots, season with salt and pepper and stir until they are a nice brownish colour. Remove to a plate and repeat the process with the onions, potatoes and lamb.

Spoon all the vegetables and lamb back into the casserole dish, placing the potatoes on top (you don't want them to get mushy). Remove all the leaves from the thyme and add to the dish. Cover with the hot lamb stock.

Cook in a preheated oven at 150°C, 300°F, Gas Mark 2 for 1 1/2 hours. Serve with crusty bread and butter.

Tip: If the juices from the stew appear too thin, thicken them by making a roux. Melt 28g (1oz) butter in a pan and whisk in 28g (1oz) flour until it forms a paste. Ladle the juices from the stew into a saucepan and slowly whisk in the roux, then pour the thickened gravy back into the stew.

Gallic Kitchen's Organic Steak Pies

The Gallic Kitchen stall, with its incredible spread of savoury and sweet pies, has become legendary in Dublin's markets. The beef pie is one of their best sellers and Sarah Webb, the owner, was kind enough to share the recipe with me. I serve it with a simple green salad.

Makes 4 x 300g (10oz) pies

4 tbsp olive oil
1 large onion, diced
650g (1lb 7oz) organic beef
    steak, chopped
salt and freshly ground
    black pepper
180g (6oz) carrots, diced

150ml (5fl oz) stout
20g (¾oz) butter
35g (1¼oz) plain flour
430g (15oz) puff pastry
1 egg, beaten
2 tsp poppy seeds

Put a tablespoon of olive oil into a large saucepan over a high heat, then add the onion and cook gently with the heat turned down low until softened.

Place a heavy-bottomed frying pan over a medium heat, add a splash of olive oil and fry the chopped beef until browned. Season with salt and pepper and add to the onions. Stir in the carrots and pour in the stout. Add more liquid, if required, to cover the ingredients – you can use beef stock or water.

Bring to the boil and then simmer gently for 1½–2 hours or until the meat is cooked and tender.

To make a roux, melt the butter in a clean saucepan over a low heat, then slowly whisk in the flour until it becomes a thick paste. Add in a spoonful of stock from the cooked meat. Strain the liquid off the meat and slowly whisk into the roux to make a thick, smooth sauce. Pour the sauce over the meat and vegetables. Stir and leave to cool.

Roll out the puff pastry on a floured surface and use two-thirds of it to line 4 individual pie tins. Fill each tin to the top with the meat filling and cover with a pastry lid. Seal and fold the edges and brush each pie with beaten egg. Sprinkle some poppy seeds on top and cook in a preheated oven at 180°C, 350°F, Gas Mark 4 for approximately 45 minutes.

Lamb Chops with Flat Parsley and Chilli Relish or Mint and Feta Relish

Lamb chops are so easy to cook. Frying them is beautifully simple and quick. Serve them with one of the delicious relishes below – they each give a real zing to lamb chops.

Serves 2

50ml (2fl oz) sunflower oil
4 loin lamb chops (2 per
    serving)

For the flat parsley and chilli relish:

1 bunch fresh flat parsley,
    chopped
1 chilli, deseeded and finely
    chopped
juice of 1 lemon
1 garlic clove, crushed

For the mint and feta relish:

50g (2oz) feta cheese,
    crumbled
1 bunch fresh mint, chopped
70ml (2½fl oz) olive oil
salt and freshly ground
    black pepper

First, prepare the relish of your choice, or both if you wish. Place all the ingredients for the parsley and chilli relish in a bowl and mix well. Alternatively, put the feta and mint in a bowl, add the olive oil, season with salt and pepper and mix well. (Feta is a very salty cheese so go easy when seasoning.)

Heat a griddle pan or frying pan until it is very hot, add the sunflower oil and, when hot, add the lamb chops. Reduce the heat to medium and cook for about 15 minutes, turning halfway. Serve with your chosen relish.

Mini Rack of Lamb with Tzatziki

These not only look beautiful when plated-up but also taste fantastic. The cumin works so well with lamb and yogurt. Make sure you get your hands on a good-quality yogurt, such as Glenilen, Glenisk or whichever dairy farmer trades at your local market.

Serves 2
2 mini racks of lamb
50ml (2fl oz) olive oil
1 tbsp whole cumin seeds
salt and freshly ground
    black pepper

For the tzatziki:
⅓ cucumber
200ml (7fl oz) natural yogurt
juice of ½ lemon
2 tsp chopped fresh mint

Rub the lamb with olive oil and then spread the cumin seeds all over the meat, pressing them into the surface. Season with salt and pepper.

Place the lamb on a baking tray and cook in a preheated oven at 170°C, 325°F, Gas Mark 3 for 20 minutes.

While the lamb is cooking, make the tzatziki. Dice the cucumber and fold into the yogurt with the lemon juice and chopped mint. Serve the lamb with the tzatziki on the side.

Pork

The poor old pig has suffered some seriously bad PR. In fact, domesticated pigs are descended from the noble wild boar - a worthy trophy for any serious huntsman. Much maligned as a 'dirty animal', pigs are, in fact, very clean and never soil the space they live in. They wallow in mud simply to keep themselves cool and to protect themselves from the sun.

Unfortunately, many farmed pigs in this country are kept in vast barns with no natural light and no access to the outdoors. Because of this intensive farming, it is necessary to pump them full of antibiotics to stop the spread of diseases like swine fever. Hugh Fearnley-Whittingstall's book *Meat* is a real revelation into both the worst and the absolute best aspects of the pork industry.

Beware of labels like 'traditional' or 'hand reared'. The only bacon you should even contemplate buying should be free range or organic. Pigs need outdoor space and ideally should be able to socialise and enjoy a varied diet. Happily, we have great pork producers right here in Ireland, such as Gubbeen Farmhouse Products, Caherbeg Farm Products and Ed Hick and Sons.

The only way you can enjoy great tasting, humanely reared bacon is to 'hunt for happy pigs' as Hugh would say, and enjoy putting pork back on your fork. Try delicious crunchy crackling, succulent slices of roast pork with sweet apple sauce, crispy bacon with melting cheese and flavoured sausages with velvety mash - is that enough inspiration for going to your local farmers' market? Oh and before you leave home, remember to take a big bag because pork freezes extremely well.

Spicy Sausage Stew with Tomatoes

At the markets in Ireland you can find really fabulous varieties of sausages, including those produced by Caherbeg, Gubbeen, Ed Hicks and Jane Russell. This stew is so simple to make it's as easy as dialling for a pizza.

Serves 4

1 tbsp olive oil
8 pork sausages (about 800g/1lb 10oz)
1 onion, chopped
1 tsp ground cumin
1 bay leaf
2 garlic cloves, roughly chopped
125ml (4½ fl oz) dry white wine
2 x 400g (14oz) cans chopped tomatoes
bunch of fresh coriander, roughly chopped
salt and freshly ground black pepper

Heat a heavy-bottomed saucepan over a medium heat. Add the olive oil and then the sausages, and cook for 8–10 minutes.

Add the onion, cumin and bay leaf to the sausages. Cook over a medium heat until the onion is soft and translucent. Add the garlic and cook for 1 minute, then pour in the white wine and continue cooking for about 2 minutes, until reduced by half. Add the tomatoes, cover the pan and cook, stirring often, for about 20 minutes until the sauce is thick.

Add the fresh coriander and check the seasoning. Serve hot with polenta, potatoes or just some crusty bread with Irish butter.

Caherbeg Pork Pie with Caramelised Apples

I first met Avril and Will Allshire of Caherbeg at the Clonakilty Market in West Cork. They have the largest outdoor free-range pig farm in Ireland. It is hard to find people like Avril and Will – their lives revolve around the well-being of their pigs and the taste of their award-winning products. Their pigs are free to root and socialise and their diet contains no meat derivatives or GM products. Thus, you can enjoy their fabulous bacon or sausages with a free conscience.

Serves 4

200g (7oz) cooking apples, e.g. Bramley, peeled, cored and sliced
15g (½oz) butter
2 tbsp honey
400g (14oz) pork sausage meat
200g (7oz) streaky unsmoked bacon, diced
salt and freshly ground black pepper
3 tbsp chopped fresh herbs (e.g. thyme, rosemary, sage)
300g (10oz) puff pastry
1 egg, beaten

First, caramelise the apples. Melt a knob of butter in a frying pan over a medium heat. Add the apples and honey and leave for 10 minutes to caramelise, tossing frequently.

Grease a casserole dish (approximately 600ml/1 pint in volume) with some butter. Place one-third of the sausage meat along the base of the dish, and scatter over the top one-third of the bacon. Season with salt and pepper, sprinkle with a few herbs, and then cover with a layer of caramelised apples. Repeat the layers in this way until they are all used up.

Roll out the pastry, brush around the edge of the dish with beaten egg and cover the pie. Prick the top with a fork and then brush all over with beaten egg (this gives a lovely golden colour).

Place the pie in a preheated oven at 170°C, 325°F, Gas Mark 3 and cook for 55–60 minutes until the pastry is puffed up and golden brown. Serve warm.

The Ferguson Family

At the top of the Gubbeen Farmhouse website is a short statement, which starts: 'Our land and the food we produce are connected'. This philosophy seems to run through the Ferguson farm, family and business. Tom Ferguson keeps a herd of cattle, the milk from which is used by his wife Giana to make the internationally famous Gubbeen cheese. The whey from the cheese is used to feed the farm's free-range pigs which are cured in son, Fingal's smokehouse, and Fingal uses his sister Clovisse's herbs in the production of the cured meats.

This is a successful, working farm, using traditional methods and employing generations of the same family to produce exceptional artisan foods. At a time when the Irish government is looking for ways to encourage younger generations to stay on family farms, the Gubbeen farm is a perfect model of how it can work.

The farm, overlooking the sea in West Cork, has been in the Ferguson family for five generations. Giana was brought up in London and spent her summers in Spain on a small farm where her family made goat's cheese. She brought this experience, along with her knowledge of the Swiss and French cheese making traditions, to Ireland when she married Tom.

After a couple of years experimenting they perfected the recipe for the now internationally famous Gubbeen cheese. It is an earthy, creamy, semi-soft cheese with a mushroomy and nutty aftertaste. People know a good thing when they taste it, and the Gubbeen went on to win many awards and was soon being exported around the globe.

The second part of the Gubbeen statement reads: 'We keep our land healthy; this produces healthy animals and crops from which we make our Gubbeen Farmhouse Produce for your family's health'. Again, this sense of connectedness filters through to every part of the farm. The milk for Giana's cheese comes from the morning milking of Tom's well-tended Friesian, Simmenthal, Jersey and Kerry cows. Clovisse's herbs and vegetables are grown completely organically. Fingal's free-range pigs have room to root and, if they are inclined, can even enjoy a grand view over the sea from their large straw-filled pens.

The Gubbeen Farmhouse produce has been a great success for the Fergusons, but they don't rest on their laurels. In the late 1980s, together with other cheese makers, Tom and Giana formed CAIS, the Irish Farmhouse Cheese-maker's Association, to establish criteria for farmhouse cheeses and a forum for the makers. Today, they continue to expand their business. Clovisse is now building an organic garden to supply farmers' markets, restaurants and shops in the area. Fingal, as well as smoking some of the Gubbeen cheese, smokes salamis, hams, continental-style sausages and bacon, mixing traditional methods with modern flavours.

For me that is a large part of the Fergusons' success; they respect craft and tradition while keeping abreast with what is modern.

Left to right: Fingal, Clovisse and Giana Ferguson and me.

Peter Ward's Baked Ham

Peter Ward and his wife, Mary, run and own the fabulous Country Choice food store in Nenagh, Co. Tipperary. They also have a stall at their local farmers' market. Peter plays a crucial role in promoting artisan food. He is chairperson of the Irish Taste Council, and convivium leader for Slow Food Tipperary. His ham is legendary – people come in droves to buy it. (So thank you, Peter, for sharing this recipe with me.) You will need to buy a free-range ham with a good layer of fat and which has been dry-cured with a mixture of salt and organic brown sugar.

Serves 12

1 full ham on the bone, approx. 2kg (5lb)
1 stick celery, roughly chopped
2 bay leaves
1 carrot, roughly chopped
16 cloves
organic brown demerara sugar

Soak the ham overnight in plenty of cold water. Drain and make a cut on the outside of the knuckle, just enough to cut the cartilage of the joint but don't cut the whole way through.

Place the ham in a large saucepan of fresh cold water. Add the celery, bay leaves, carrot and 4 cloves. Bring to a fast boil and skim off any foam. Reduce to a gentle simmer and cook gently for about 3 hours or until the skin blisters and feels soft to the touch. If you own a range or Aga, you can put the pot into the warming oven.

Leave the ham to cool in the cooking water before removing the skin carefully. Make sure that you do not take away the fat from the meat. Score the surface diagonally with a sharp knife and stud deeply with a clove in each diamond shape.

Rub the brown sugar gently into the surface of the ham. Cover the exposed side of the ham with foil and then bake in a preheated oven at 200°C, 400°F, Gas Mark 6 for 20 minutes or until golden brown.

Tip: Ham is delicious glazed. You can use any jam or jelly - a spiced apple or redcurrant would be ideal. Just before you place the ham in the oven, cover with your jam or jelly of choice. Every 5 minutes during the cooking, scoop the juices that have slid down the ham back over it again - this is called basting.

Gubbeen Chorizo and Bean Stew

This recipe was given to me by Fingal Ferguson of the Gubbeen Smokehouse (see pages 76–77). It is a warm and comforting dish, and the perfect supper for a cold, windy evening.

Serves 4

50ml (2fl oz) olive oil
400g (14oz) chorizo
    sausage, skin removed
    and roughly chopped
1 red pepper, deseeded
    and diced
1 onion, diced
2 garlic cloves, crushed

1 tsp paprika
400g (14oz) can chopped
    tomatoes
2 x 400g (14oz) cans
    butter beans
salt and freshly ground
    black pepper

Place a flameproof casserole dish or large saucepan over a medium heat and add the olive oil. When the oil is hot, add the chorizo and cook until crisp. Stir in the red pepper, onion and garlic and reduce the heat.

Cover the dish and leave to simmer for 10 minutes. Add the paprika, tomatoes, beans and season with salt and pepper. Stir well and leave to simmer, uncovered, for 15 minutes.

My favourite way to eat this dish is on my lap with a huge chunk of white sourdough bread smothered with Irish butter (see page 27). The bread helps me scoop out all the juices and, as they say, 'scrape the end of the barrel'.

Isabelle Sheridan's Pork and Prune Terrine

Isabelle Sheridan has an incredible charcuterie and farmhouse cheese stall called 'On the Pig's Back' in the English Market, Cork. She makes all her own terrines and pâtés. This terrine is the best! It is an original recipe she created for her stall, from a basic country recipe handed down by her mother. After 14 years, it is still a favourite seller in Cork and has been copied many times since!

Serves 12

100g (3½ oz) whole prunes (e.g. *pruneaux d'Agen*)
500g (1lb 2 oz) fresh pork belly, minced
250g (9 oz) lean pork, diced
250g (9 oz) pork liver, minced
1 large onion, finely chopped
1 garlic clove, crushed
3 eggs, beaten

salt and cracked pepper
2 pinches of 4-spices (*quatre épices*)
1 pinch of ground coriander
100ml of brandy
50ml (2fl oz) olive oil
6-8 rashers streaky bacon, stretched out thin using the back of a knife

Put the prunes in a saucepan, cover with water and bring slowly to simmering point. Remove the pan from the heat and set aside to cool before draining and stoning the prunes. Keep the cooking liquid.

Mix together the minced pork belly, diced pork, processed liver and chopped onion in a bowl (or use a food processor). Stir in the prune liquid and the whole, stoned prunes, keeping back two for the garnish. Now add the garlic, beaten eggs, 3 pinches of salt, 1 pinch of cracked pepper, the ground spices and brandy. Mix until everything is incorporated.

Heat a frying pan and add the oil. Fry a small sample of the mixture to check the seasoning – you cannot rectify it later. A terrine is eaten cold, so the seasoning should be a little salty for your taste while it's hot. The after taste should be nice and long, so don't hesitate to add more spices and coriander to the mixture if you think they're necessary.

Line a 900g (2lb) loaf tin with some of the stretched streaky bacon rashers, overlapping them so that they hang over the edges of the dish. Spoon the mixture into it. Bring the overhanging rashers over the top, and then use the rest of the rashers to ensure that the mixture is completely covered. Garnish with the reserved prunes, cut in halves. Cover tightly with kitchen foil and place in a bain-marie, or stand in a roasting pan half-filled with water.

Cook in a preheated oven at 180°C, 350°F, Gas Mark 4 for 1½ hours. Leave to cool for 20 minutes, cover with foil and then place a board and weight on the top of the terrine to compact the layers, allowing the terrine to cut easily. Leave to cool to room temperature, and then chill in the fridge overnight.

The next day, un-mould the terrine and wrap it in cling film. It is best left in the fridge for two or three days before being eaten. Serve sliced as a starter with bread, a green salad and onion marmalade, or use in a cold meat platter, a snack with crackers, after pub parties or at picnics. It also makes fabulous sandwiches!

Chicken

Roasted organic chicken with delicious crispy skin and succulent meat; velvety smooth liver pâté; cold chicken sandwiches with home-made mayonnaise; or comforting chicken broth or casserole on a cold winter evening – all sounds very good doesn't it? Moreover, the recipes couldn't be easier, even for the most inexperienced of cooks. But before you go out and buy chicken, think carefully about exactly what type of chicken you're buying.

Free-range chicken is more expensive than standard broiler chicken (chicken that is intensively reared for meat), and organic more expensive still, but it's well worth the extra money. Organic chicken is still cheaper than the cheapest steak, plus it goes a great deal further. Two chickens will provide three meals for a family of six, and you can use the carcass to make stock for soups, stews, casseroles and curries (see page 126).

Shopping for a good chicken can be quite confusing as there are many different labels. Here's a brief guide:

- 'Corn fed' is deceptive: the chicken will have been fed on corn or maize, which is a good alternative to fishmeal or GM feed but, unless the label states free range, it has still been reared intensively.
- 'Free range' means that chickens have access to outdoors as well as shelter. It doesn't, however, mean that they've been given GM- or antibiotic-free feed or that the slaughter and transport is any better than broilers.
- So that leaves 'organic' – this is the one you should always choose. Organic means that the chickens have access to outdoors where they can forage and scratch, and that they are given feed free of antibiotics and GM ingredients.

The fact is that we are eating too much intensively reared chicken, so why not try an experiment? Buy an organic chicken just once a fortnight and balance out the extra money you spend by purchasing other not-so-expensive foods, like lamb shanks, pulses, mackerel and seasonal vegetables. You will not only be blown away by a delicious meal and the nutritional benefits of varying your diet, but meal times will become much more exciting! In doing this you'll exercise your consumer clout and boycott broiler chicken, helping to promote animal welfare. Now you can sit back and enjoy your meat with a conscience as clear as the juices running into the roasting tin.

Roast Chicken with Preserved Lemons, Fresh Thyme and Roasted Potatoes

A roast chicken can be transformed by delicious home-made preserved lemons (see page 185). However, you can use regular lemons or buy ready-preserved ones instead. I assure you that your feelings for this dish will become an everlasting love affair.

Serves 4
1 chicken, 1.5–2 kg (2½–5 lb)
20g (³⁄₄ oz) butter
4 sprigs fresh thyme, leaves
    removed
salt and freshly ground
    black pepper
2 preserved lemons
6 waxy potatoes, peeled
    and thickly sliced

Rub the chicken with butter, then sprinkle with the thyme leaves and season with salt and pepper. Cut the preserved lemons into large strips and lay over the chicken. Place the thyme sprigs in the cavity.

   Place the chicken in a roasting pan and cook in a preheated oven at 180°C, 350°F, Gas Mark 4 for 1½ hours. Arrange the sliced potatoes around the chicken in the pan and spoon all the juices from the chicken over them. Cook for a further 40 minutes. To check that the chicken is cooked, pierce the meat with a skewer behind the leg – the juices should run clear.

Chicken Liver Pâté

When I was a chef at Ballymaloe House, this pâté was one of the most popular dishes on the menu. So when I took a stall at the local farmers' market in Midleton, I used to make kilos of it to sell. Everyone loves it!

Serves 10
450g (1lb) butter (softened)
675g (1½ lb) chicken livers,
    cleaned
2 tbsp brandy
1 garlic clove
2 tsp thyme

For the caramelised onions:
20g (¾ oz) butter
2 onions, sliced
1 tbsp brown mustard seeds

Melt a knob of the butter in a frying pan and add the chicken livers. Cook over a medium heat for about 15 minutes, stirring occasionally. When the chicken livers are cooked, there should be no trace of redness in the meat. Transfer them to a food processor.

Add the brandy, garlic and thyme to the frying pan and deglaze by scraping up all the tiny pieces of meat and juices from the livers using a whisk- the bottom of the pan is where the real flavour is! Add the brandy mixture to the food processor and blend with the livers. Leave to cool.

While the livers are cooling, make the caramelised onions. Melt the butter in a saucepan and stir in the onions. Reduce the heat, cover the pan and leave to sweat for about 5 minutes. Then remove the lid, turn up the heat and stir in the mustard seeds. Continue cooking until the onions have softened and become rich and brown in colour. Leave to cool.

Slowly add the remaining butter to the cooled chicken liver mixture and mix until all the butter has blended. Fold in the caramelised onions.

Transfer the chicken liver and onion mixture to a large dish and leave to set in the fridge for at least 3 hours. This pâté is delicious served with hot crunchy white bread.

Chicken Wings with Sour Cream

Not everyone can afford to buy a whole organic chicken, so for the days when you are feeling a pinch in your pocket and a craving for chicken these wings are the answer. I can buy four for one Euro at my local market.

Serves 2
1 tbsp cayenne pepper
70ml (2 ½ fl oz) olive oil
12 organic chicken wings
salt and freshly ground
    black pepper
sour cream, to serve

Put the cayenne pepper in a bowl and mix with the olive oil so you end up with a sticky, slightly runny paste. Season the chicken wings with salt and pepper and pour the cayenne pepper paste over them in a bowl. Mix until the wings are nicely coated.

Place the wings on a baking sheet and cook in a preheated oven at 180°C, 350°F, Gas Mark 4 for 30 minutes until crisp and golden brown. Serve with a big bowl of sour cream for dipping the wings into.

Roasted Spicy Chicken with Almonds and Chorizo Served with Spicy Potato Wedges

This recipe is fantastic if you are having lots of people round for dinner, just multiply the quantities accordingly. Silky chicken, spicy chorizo, crunchy almonds and cooling sour cream ... are you getting hungry?

Serves 4
4 tbsp olive oil
1 organic chicken, 1.5–2 kg (2½–5 lb), jointed into 8 pieces
10cm (4in) piece of chorizo, skinned and roughly chopped
1 head garlic, peeled, cloves left whole
2 x 400g (14oz) cans chopped tomatoes
15 Kalamata olives, roughly chopped
4 garlic cloves, peeled
4 tbsp flaked almonds
1 tbsp paprika
salt and freshly ground black pepper
sour cream, to serve

For the spicy potato wedges:
700g (2lb 9oz) potatoes, wash, leave unpeeled and cut into long thin wedges
50ml (2fl oz) olive oil
1 tbsp cayenne pepper
1 tbsp paprika

Place a roasting pan over a medium heat and add the olive oil. When the oil is hot, add the chicken pieces and lightly brown, then add the chorizo and allow to crisp. Toss in all of the remaining ingredients (except the sour cream) and season with salt and pepper. Place in a preheated oven at 200°C, 400°F, Gas Mark 6 and cook for 45 minutes.

Put the potato wedges in a large bowl with the oil, spices and seasoning. Toss well until the potatoes are coated with the mixture, and place on a baking tray. Cook in a preheated oven at 200°C, 400°F, Gas Mark 6 for 30–35 minutes. Serve with the chicken and a big dollop of sour cream.

Ummera Smoked Chicken Paella

I came up with this recipe when I had a stall in Courtmacsherry, next to Anthony Creswell, owner of the nearby Ummera Smokehouse. While I was there a television company telephoned to ask me to come up with a recipe that same day, so I grabbed Anthony's smoked chicken, Fingal Ferguson's chorizo, some freshly caught mussels and prawns, a bunch of seaweed and headed home to experiment. At the markets, we have all the great ingredients to create an Irish version of this classic Spanish dish.

Serves 10

8 tbsp olive oil
150g (5oz) chorizo, sliced
2 onions, chopped
4 garlic cloves, crushed
8 tomatoes, roughly
    chopped
1 red pepper, deseeded
    and sliced
270g (9½oz) paella rice
salt and freshly ground black
    pepper
1 tsp paprika
1 tsp turmeric

800ml (1⅓ pints) hot
    chicken stock
500g (1lb 2oz) live mussels
    (see prep method on
    page 44)
6 large prawns, whole, raw
    and unshelled
300g (10oz) Ummera
    smoked chicken, sliced
50g (2oz) Desmond cheese
    (or Parmesan), grated
1 lemon, cut into wedges

Heat a large paella pan or heavy-bottomed frying pan, about 30cm (12in) diameter, over a medium heat and add the olive oil. When hot, fry the chorizo until crispy. Add the onions, garlic, tomatoes and red pepper, and cook for 15 minutes, stirring occasionally.

Stir the rice into the pan and season with salt and pepper. Add the paprika and turmeric, followed by the hot stock, and leave to simmer for 10 minutes. Add the mussels and prawns and simmer for a further 5 minutes. Scatter the pieces of smoked chicken over the rice, followed by the Desmond cheese. Leave to simmer for 3 minutes, then cover for a further 10 minutes or until the mussels have opened completely. Serve with lemon wedges.

Vegetables

Buying Seasonally

Vegetables often seem to take a bit of a back seat, a side dish or an accompaniment to the main attraction. Well, all that is changing. While Ireland still, to my mind, grows some of the best potatoes in the world we are no longer just a nation of potato growers. We grow everything from squashes and kales to heirloom tomatoes, sprouting broccolis and more. Stalls at our farmers' markets are groaning with locally grown, seasonal vegetables and most are sold out by midday. In fact, Café Paradiso, Denis Cotter and Bridget Healy's superb vegetarian restaurant (which has just been voted *the* best restaurant in Ireland), sources most of its vegetables locally from Irish grower, Ultan Walsh.

So, when today's global marketplace allows us to buy foods grown virtually anywhere in the world all year round, why should we choose to buy locally produced, seasonal fare? Well, the food hasn't travelled from the other side of the world. Because it's local, it's fresher and tastes better as a result. You and your family will enjoy the benefits of eating vegetables picked for optimum flavour and nutritional value, and that haven't been chemically treated so that they last an epic journey.

Just look at tomatoes. Two thirds of the tomatoes we eat are imported. Imported tomatoes are picked while they are still green and artificially ripened using ethylene gas, hence the tough skin and watery, flavourless flesh. Yet, in season, we have an abundance of great Irish tomatoes of infinitely better quality, texture and taste. Local growers can choose varieties with the best taste and texture because they will be on sale the day after they are picked. They can also let their tomatoes ripen on the vine, which gives them a rich flavour and allows the nutrients to fully develop.

Here's another reason to buy local, seasonal and fresh produce: packaging. Salad that is bagged up and transported loses many of its valuable nutrients. Compare that to vegetables and salad pulled straight from the ground, when they are fully ripe, and then boxed and transported the same day to a local stall.

With such a fantastic range of vegetables grown in Ireland today it has never been easier to obtain high-quality produce. Buying at the markets puts you, the consumer, back in touch with farmers, so you know where your food is coming from and how it was produced. It also puts you back in touch with the seasons. Above all, it means you and your family are eating vegetables that taste better and are much better for you.

Pandy

This is an old Cork expression for 'mashed potatoes'. Pandy is deliciously creamy and rich in taste, and smooth as silk! I can sit and eat bowls upon bowls of it on a cold autumn evening. It is the ultimate comfort food.

Serves 4
1kg (2lb 4oz) potatoes,
    washed
100ml (3½ fl oz) warm milk
a knob of butter
salt and freshly ground
    black pepper

Place the potatoes in a saucepan – the largest ones at the bottom – and fill halfway with water. Cover the pan and place over a high heat. When the water begins to boil, drain off about half, leaving just enough for the potatoes to steam.

When the potatoes are cooked – after about 30-40 minutes depending on size – peel (hold them in a tea towel) and place in a warm bowl. Mash them, gradually adding the warm milk, then add a knob of butter and season to taste with salt and pepper.

Try these delicious variations:
- For a mustard mash, fold in 1 tablespoon mustard powder and 1 tablespoon mustard seeds.
- For Colcannon, add 2 chopped spring onions (scallions) to the warm milk and continue as above.
- For sweet mash add in 6 tablespoons of caramelised onions.
- For cheesy mash add in 6 tablespoons of grated mature Cheddar.
- And for all you fun-loving St Patrick's Day followers, add in 4 tablespoons of finely chopped fresh parsley for the green effect!

Tip: Cooking the potatoes in their skins keeps in all the delicious flavour and nutrients. It also allows the butter and milk to be easily absorbed once peeled (because the potatoes are very dry from having been cooked with their skins on) – ensuring a wonderful smooth mash.

Roast Pumpkin with Rosemary

In Autumn you will find vegetable stalls in Ireland stacked with pumpkins; all sorts of wonderful varieties like 'small sugar' and 'Jack be little'. It's a wonderfully versatile vegetable and is delicious roasted, in soup or in pies.

Serves 8

1 kg (1lb 2oz) pumpkin, cut into wedges, deseeded
50ml (2fl oz) olive oil
2 sprigs fresh rosemary, broken up
salt and black pepper

Place the pumpkin wedges on a roasting tray with a slurp of olive oil, the rosemary and some sea salt and pepper. Pop into a preheated oven at 170°C, 325°F, Gas Mark 3 and cook for about 40 minutes until tender.

Tip: The skin is perfectly edible, but can be peeled off after roasting if preferred.

Honey-glazed Winter Roots

This glaze is sheer glamour for vegetables. It makes them look, taste and smell fabulous, and enhances their natural sweetness.

Serves 4

2 carrots
2 parsnips
1 tbsp honey
1 tbsp brown sugar
50ml (2fl oz) extra virgin olive oil
salt and freshly ground black pepper

Cut the carrots and parsnips into wedges and place them in a roasting pan or ovenproof dish. Drizzle over the honey, sprinkle with sugar and olive oil, and season with salt and pepper.

Cook in a preheated oven at 170°C, 325°F, Gas Mark 3 for 40 minutes, stirring occasionally to coat the vegetables evenly with the glaze. Serve hot.

The Irish Farmers' Market Cookbook

Spicy Green Beans with Tomatoes

This recipe is fabulous served with lamb, beef, fish - anything really!

Serves 4
50ml (2fl oz) olive oil
1 onion, thinly sliced
2.5cm (1 in) fresh root ginger, peeled
    and finely chopped
2 garlic cloves, crushed
1 red tiger chilli, finely chopped
400g (14oz) can chopped tomatoes
500g (1lb 2oz) green beans
salt and freshly ground black pepper

Place a saucepan over a medium heat and add the olive oil. Add the onion, ginger, garlic and chilli, then cover the pan and sweat for 2 minutes. Stir in the tomatoes and simmer for a further 2 minutes.

While the tomatoes are simmering, tip the green beans into a pan of boiling water and cook for 3-4 minutes until tender. Drain and add to the spicy tomatoes. Check the seasoning and serve hot.

Slow-cooked Red Cabbage with Apples

This way of cooking red cabbage is great for serving with lamb, pork or beef roasts.

Serves 10

900g (2lb) red cabbage, shredded
   (discard the tough outer leaves)
salt and freshly ground black pepper
450g (1lb) Bramley cooking apples,
   peeled, cored and finely chopped
1/4 whole nutmeg, freshly grated
3 tbsp dark brown soft sugar
3 tbsp white wine vinegar
10g (1/3 oz) butter

Arrange a layer of the shredded cabbage in the base of a casserole dish and season lightly with salt and pepper. Add a layer of chopped apples with a sprinkling of nutmeg and sugar. Continue layering up the red cabbage and apple in this way until everything is used up. Pour in the vinegar and dot with butter on top.

Put a tight-fitting lid on the casserole and let it cook very slowly in a preheated oven at 150°C, 300°F, Gas Mark 2 for 2-2¼ hours, stirring once or twice during cooking.

Asparagus with Hollandaise Sauce on Toast

If you have locally grown organic asparagus, fresh free-range eggs and good-quality bread, this is one of the most delicious meals you can possibly experience.

Serves 2
50ml (2fl oz) olive oil
8 asparagus spears
salt and freshly ground black pepper
200g (7 oz) butter
4 egg yolks (reserve the whites for the
    pavlova recipe on page 200)
juice of ½ lemon
4 slices good-quality bread (white
    sourdough is best, see page 27)

If you have a griddle pan, place it over a high heat and add the olive oil. When the oil is hot, lay the asparagus spears on top. Leave to cook for 2 minutes on each side and season with salt and pepper. If you don't have a griddle pan, fill a saucepan with water, about one-third full, and place over a high heat. When the water begins to boil, drop in the asparagus and cook for about 4 minutes until the stems are just tender.

To make the hollandaise sauce, place a small saucepan over a very low heat. Add the butter and leave to melt slowly. Whisk in the egg yolks, one at a time, until they are well amalgamated. Remove from the heat and whisk in the lemon juice. Check the seasoning.

Toast the bread and divide them between 2 plates. Place 2 asparagus spears on each slice of toast and smother with the hollandaise sauce. Serve immediately.

Tip: If your hollandaise sauce curdles, remove the pan immediately from the heat, add a couple of ice cubes and keep whisking.

Potato, Tomato and Fresh Ginger Curry

This curry is fantastic - just be careful not to over-cook it or the potatoes will go to mush!

Serves 4

500g (1lb 2oz) potatoes, washed and left whole if they are small and cut in half if they are big
2 tsp cumin seeds
50ml (2fl oz) olive oil
2 onions, chopped
4 garlic cloves, crushed
5cm (2 in) piece fresh root ginger, peeled and crushed
1 tsp turmeric
1 aubergine, cut into wedges
2 courgettes, cut into wedges
450g (1lb) crushed tomatoes
2 tsp ground coriander
3 tbsp natural yogurt
salt and freshly ground black pepper

Put the potatoes in a saucepan, fill halfway with water and place over a high heat. When the water starts to boil, reduce the heat, pour off half the liquid and then simmer until the potatoes are slightly tender. Leave to cool and cut into wedges.

Dry-roast the cumin seeds in a frying pan for about 2 minutes. Place a saucepan over a medium heat, add a splash of olive oil and pour in the potatoes, onions, garlic, ginger, turmeric and roasted cumin seeds. Cook until the potatoes are golden, stirring all the time. Then remove to a plate and keep warm.

Pour the remaining olive oil into the pan and allow it to heat up before adding the aubergine and courgettes. Cook for 5 minutes. Return the spicy potato mixture to the pan and stir in the tomatoes, coriander and yogurt. Season with salt and pepper and leave to simmer over a low heat for about 10 minutes. Serve with basmati rice.

Caroline Robinson

Caroline Robinson has a farm with her husband Eddie in Templemartin where they grow chemical-free fruit and vegetables. She sells at the markets as well as direct to the customer – putting together weekly orders of fruit and vegetables, which customers collect from the end of her farm road.

Caroline is also a food activist and helps organise meetings about food-related issues for the Cork Free Choice Consumer Group. Topics of discussion are diverse:

Caroline Robinson at Coal Quay Market in Cork City.

one week there may be a guest speaker talking about coffee and the Fair Trade movement, the following week could be a talk on turning food waste into superb compost. She also finds time, somehow, to chair the Irish Food Market Traders Association, promoting markets throughout Ireland and negotiating with the authorities on behalf of food traders.

Caroline is also passionately interested in finding solutions for the consequences of 'peak oil'. In very simple terms, peak oil refers to the expected huge decline in worldwide oil production, which will lead to massive global shortages. Caroline and Eddie are experimenting with ways to produce the maximum amount of food by using very little energy in the form of diesel for tractors, pumping water, etc, and are constantly testing the most efficient methods for growing vegetables without chemical fertilisers or pesticides.

Caroline Robinson: grower, activist, promoter, environmentalist. One thing you know is you can trust her produce completely but if you want to eat it, get there quick – she is usually sold out by midday.

Roasted Beetroot with Yogurt and Toasted Almonds

When beetroot is in season, I am surprised that my skin doesn't turn purple, I eat so much of it! Roasted and served with yogurt, crunchy almonds and peppery rocket, it's great for lunch or as part of a buffet for a barbecue.

Serves 6

8 beetroots
50ml (2fl oz) olive oil
salt and freshly ground
    black pepper
70g (2¼oz) flaked almonds

100ml (3½fl oz) natural yogurt
bunch of fresh rocket

Scrub the beetroots and cut off the tails. Place them in a roasting pan, then drizzle with olive oil and season with salt and pepper.

Place in a preheated oven at 180°C, 350°F, Gas Mark 4 and cook for 40 minutes. Meanwhile, dry-roast the flaked almonds in a frying pan, tossing them all the time until you get a lovely golden colour.

Cool the cooked beetroots slightly, then cut into wedges and place in a serving bowl. Pour the yogurt and almonds over the top and fold in the rocket. Serve cold or lukewarm.

Tips:

- Early beetroot greens are so tender that you can put them in a salad.
- Look out for different varieties. You can buy white and golden beetroots and even a variety with pink and white stripes called candy beetroot.
- Only peel beetroot if it is rough around the top, by the stems. If you do have to peel it, cook it first as this will preserve more of the nutrients.
- The freshest beetroots should not be blemished or wrinkly, nor the taproot dried out. White-grey patches around the shoulders are absolutely normal.
- Don't wash beetroot before storing it. It is best kept in a plastic bag in the fridge. Roots will keep for up to three weeks this way. In the old days, cooks used to pack roots in peat which would keep them fresh well into the winter. The sugar content acted as a sort of anti-freeze! However, beetroot should never be frozen.

Ratatouille

This colourful, traditional French dish is as healthy as it is hearty.
If you're feeling creative, use this recipe as a base and add your
own choice of vegetables for variety.

Serves 4
1 aubergine, sliced
1 courgette, sliced
1 red pepper, deseeded and cut
   into wedges
1 red onion, sliced
2 garlic cloves, crushed
400g (14 oz) can plum tomatoes
salt and freshly ground
   black pepper
1 bunch of fresh basil or 4 sprigs
   fresh rosemary, roughly
   chopped

Put all the vegetables together with the garlic and tomatoes in a roasting dish, and
season with salt and pepper.

Place in a preheated oven at 170°C, 325°F, Gas Mark 3 and cook for 30 minutes
or until the vegetables are tender. If you are using rosemary, add it to the dish
before cooking, but basil should be added just before serving.

Tip: Try adding cooked pork, chicken, beef, lamb or any kind of fish to make this
into a wonderful hearty stew.

Cashel Blue, Caramelised Onion and Thyme Pizza

Once you've got over the scary thought of making your own pizza base, you're free to experiment with all different types of toppings, such as classic fresh tomatoes with cheese or spicy chorizo and Parmesan. However, my favourite topping is this combination.

Makes 1 pizza, serves 2

6g (1/3oz) fresh yeast
200ml (7fl oz) tepid water
100g (3 1/2 oz) plain white flour
20g (3/4oz) butter
2 medium onions, peeled,
    quartered and sliced thinly
50ml (2fl oz) olive oil

150g (5oz) Cashel Blue
    cheese, or other strong
    blue cheese
2 tsp finely chopped fresh
    thyme
salt and freshly ground
    black pepper

Put the fresh yeast into a small bowl and cover with 100ml of the water and leave to dissolve for 5 minutes. Place the flour in a bowl and make a well in the centre and pour the dissolved yeast into the centre. Then add a pinch of salt and mix in the flour from the sides. Add approximately 100ml of water and mix into a dough. Tip out onto a lightly floured surface and knead the dough by pushing the dough away from you with the back of your hand until you reach a light consistency. Place the dough back in the bowl, cover with a tea towel and place in a warm place for approximately 3 hours to allow the dough to rise.

While the dough is rising you can get your toppings ready. Place a saucepan over a medium heat and add in the butter, when the butter has melted add in the onions, cover and leave to sweat for about 10 minutes. Then remove the lid, turn up the heat and stir the onions until they become lovely and brown. Tip the onions into a bowl and leave to cool.

Preheat the oven to at 180°C, 350°F, Gas Mark 4. When the dough has risen tip out onto a floured board and roll out to make a circular pizza shape, I like my pizzas thin so I roll it to about 5mm (1/4in) thick. Then brush the pizza base with some olive oil, spread the onions out all over the base, crumble the blue cheese on top, and spinkle over the finely chopped thyme. Season with salt and pepper, then place in the oven for 20 minutes.

Aubergine and Goat's Cheese Rolls

These are great as a canapé or for a starter. They are not only simple to make but they look and taste fantastic too.

Serves 4 (makes 12 in total)
3 large aubergines
salt and freshly ground
    black pepper
olive oil, for frying
70g (2¼oz) flaked almonds
100g (3½oz) soft goat's cheese
    (e.g. I prefer Ardsallgh or St. Ola)
bunch of fresh rocket

Cut the aubergines lengthways into 1cm (½in) thick slices. Lay them on a cooling rack and sprinkle over some salt. Leave for about 10 minutes and then turn them over and repeat on the other side. This takes out all the extra moisture so they don't become soggy after being fried. You will notice that drops of water appear on the aubergine - wipe them off with a clean cloth or paper towel.

Place a frying pan over a high heat and pour in the olive oil, about 2.5cm (1in) deep. When the oil is hot, fry the aubergines until light brown on both sides. Transfer to a cooling rack and leave to drain.

Place a dry frying pan over a medium heat and lightly toast the flaked almonds, tossing them all the time.

Place the aubergines on a board and add a small spoonful of soft goat's cheese to the top of each one with a sprinkle of flaked almonds. Season with salt and pepper, add a few sprigs of rocket and roll up like a sausage roll.

Pasta, Soups
& Salads

Cooking Pasta

Fresh pasta versus dried pasta is an age-old debate. Dried is convenient to store and has more 'bite'; fresh pasta is softer and has a silkier texture. It comes down to personal taste but I'd always plump for fresh. Thankfully, really good, fresh pasta is available at many farmers' markets in Ireland. If you think about it, we produce great flour and our free-range eggs are fantastic so it makes perfect sense!

Making pasta is not an exact science. There are variables such as egg size, so concentrate on getting the consistency of the dough right, I tend to keep it firm because it is much easier to roll. Allow the pasta to dry for an hour or two before you cook it, because this will stop it sticking together when cooked. If you're using eggs in your pasta dough it needs to be eaten on the same day.

Cooking fresh pasta is much quicker than dried – really no more than three minutes, check it every minute or so. Cook it in a big pot and make sure you have plenty of boiling water or it will go 'gloopy'. The water should be on a rolling boil before you put the pasta in. It is best when slightly firm or 'al dente' (literally translated as 'to the tooth'). To check it's ready take a strand from the pot and chew. It should be tender but not mushy.

Try serving fresh pasta with sage fried in fresh butter – a tip I picked up in Italy and heartbreakingly good!

Tips for Cooking Fresh Pasta

- No need for olive oil in the water when cooking as it makes no difference. Instead, hold back one cup of the cooking water and stir this into the cooked, drained pasta, then drain again. This keeps the pasta from sticking together.
- Only cook fresh pasta when everyone is sitting at the table, as it cooks exceptionally quickly, loses flavour quickly and does not reheat well.
- Fresh pasta should be cooked in a very large saucepan of boiling water with one teaspoon of salt.
- For servings of 4–6, drop the fresh pasta into boiling water and cover with a lid. Once the water has come back to the boil, leave for 30 seconds then drain.
- Grate the fresh Parmesan just before you are about to eat as it begins to lose its flavour very quickly after being grated.

Iago's Tagliatelle with Bacon and Mushrooms

Iago is a wonderful stall in The English Market, Cork, which is run and owned by Sean and Josephine Calder-Pott. They sell a mouth-watering range of cheeses and beautiful olive oils, but what lures me to their stall time and time again is their freshly made pasta.

Serves 4

60g (2oz) butter
1 garlic clove, crushed
120g (4½ oz) Gubbeen lardons or diced smoked streaky bacon
250g (9oz) mixed mushrooms
200ml (7fl oz) crème fraîche
450g (1lb) tagliatelle, cooked al dente
salt and freshly ground black pepper
70g (2¼oz) Gabriel or Grana cheese (or Parmesan)

Melt the butter in a pan, add the garlic and cook until soft but not browned. Increase the heat before adding in the bacon and the mushrooms. Add a little more butter if needed and fry until cooked.

Pour in the crème fraîche and bring to the boil. Simmer and reduce a little. Add in the cooked tagliatelle and heat through. Season with salt and pepper.

Serve immediately with grated Gabriel cheese or a good Grana (use Parmesan if you can't get hold of these).

Fresh Pasta

I used to make fresh pasta to sell at the markets. Visitors to my house would be greeted by tagliatelle hanging from clothes horses and backs of chairs. It was like a pasta wonderland, and probably one of the happiest times of my life!

Makes approx. 1kg (2lb 4oz)
500g (1lb 2oz) durum pasta flour
a large pinch of salt
7 medium eggs
semolina flour, for dusting

Place the flour, salt and eggs in a food processor and blend the ingredients together until a dough forms. Place the dough on a floured board and knead until smooth. Separate the dough into 6 balls, cover with a tea towel and allow to rest in a cool place or in the fridge for 30 minutes.

If you have a pasta machine, set it up and push the dough through the rollers 8 times. With each pass through the rollers reduce the setting, until you reach the final setting. Be careful that your pasta does not break as you should now have a long thin sheet. If you don't have a pasta maker you need to roll the dough out very thinly with a rolling pin. (This can be hard as it breaks easily – I would highly recommend buying a pasta maker as they are inexpensive and so useful.) Then, dust lightly with semolina flour and hang over a clean clothes horse or something similar for 10 minutes. Store in the fridge, and eat within 2 days.

To make lasagne sheets, cut the pasta into suitably sized rectangles. To make tagliatelle, cut into 1cm (½ in) thick strips. For tagliolini, cut into ½ cm (¼in) strips.

Tip: You can colour your pasta with spinach, basil, tomato or even squid ink for black pasta (keep an eye on the quantity of flour you're using, you may need slightly more or less). You can also flavour it with different herbs, such as basil or coriander.

Ravioli of Frank's Smoked Salmon and Jane's Goat's Cheese

Frank Hederman's smoked salmon and Jane Murphy's goat's cheese (see pages 36–7 and 172) are delicious together, and this makes a simple dish for dinner or lunch. If you don't have the time to make the fresh pasta then you can buy it at a good food shop or Italian deli.

Serves 6

1 quantity basic pasta (see page 119)
150g (5oz) soft goat's cheese (Ardsallagh
    if you can get it)
salt and freshly ground black pepper
80g (3oz) Desmond cheese (or Parmesan)
extra virgin olive oil, for drizzling
150g (5oz) smoked salmon, cut into pieces
fresh rocket leaves, to garnish

Cut the pasta into strips about 10cm (4in) wide, and place a teaspoon of goat's cheese at 7.5cm (3in) intervals down the strip. Season the smoked salmon with salt and pepper and place a teaspoon of it on top of the cheese.

Fold the pasta over the filling and press down around it to seal it in. Cut out the pasta parcels with a sharp knife and crimp the edges with a fork to ensure that the filling doesn't ooze out during cooking.

Put a large saucepan of salted water over a high heat and bring to the boil. Drop in the ravioli and cook for 5 minutes, then drain well and arrange on 6 serving plates. Grate some Desmond cheese over the top and drizzle with olive oil. Season with salt and pepper and dress with rocket leaves. Yum!

Tagliatelle with Roast Butternut Squash, Parmesan and Watercress

I absolutely love this recipe. If you have never cooked squash before, this is your chance! It is so good that I serve it up to accompany lamb or chicken.

Serves 4

600g (1lb 5oz) butternut squash (or 400g/14oz peeled and seeds removed)
70ml (2¼fl oz) olive oil
salt and freshly ground black pepper
200ml (7fl oz) crème fraîche

75g (2½oz) Parmesan cheese, grated
500g (1lb 2oz) fresh tagliatelle (see page 119)
handful of fresh watercress or rocket

Halve the butternut squash and peel the outer skin (get a good peeler for easy work). Slice the flesh into quarters and scoop out the seeds. Cut into 1cm (½in) cubes and place on a roasting tray. Drizzle with olive oil and season with salt and pepper.

Cook in a preheated oven at 180°C, 350°F, Gas Mark 4 for 35 minutes (you will notice the squash getting wrinkly). Stir once every 10 minutes to coat the squash nicely with the oil.

Remove from the oven and stir in the crème fraîche. Scatter with grated Parmesan and 1 teaspoon black pepper (this balances the saltiness of the Parmesan) and return to the oven for 2–3 minutes until melted.

Put a large saucepan of salted water over a high heat, and when it comes to the boil drop in the fresh pasta. It will only take 3 minutes to cook - it overcooks really easily. Drain off all the water and rinse the pasta in a colander with hot water.

Transfer to a big serving bowl and fold through the squash, crème fraîche and Parmesan. Just before eating, fold in the watercress or rocket – this gives a lighter, fresher taste to the dish.

Tagliolini with Sage Butter

If you ever go to northern Italy, you must go to Bra. This is where the Slow Food movement began and it has an official Slow Food restaurant called Boccondivino. Every time I go to Bra my great friend Sebastiano Sardo, an advisor on Artisan producers for Slow Food, takes me there and I always have this dish. The only difference between this recipe and theirs is that they use 20 egg yolks for the same quantity of flour!

Serves 4
salt and freshly ground
    black pepper
500g (1lb 2 oz) fresh tagliolini
    (see page 119)
1 large bunch of fresh sage,
    chopped
50g (2oz) butter

Put a large saucepan of salted hot water over a high heat. As soon as it comes to a rolling boil, throw in all the pasta and cook for 3 minutes. It should be al dente (literally 'to the tooth', which means it should have a little bite to it). Keep an eye on as it's easy to overcook.

Drain off all the cooking water and rinse the pasta in a colander with hot water. Transfer the pasta to a big serving bowl.

For the sage butter, place a frying pan over a medium heat and add the butter, when the butter has melted add the sage and cook until it is slightly crispy. Pour the sage butter over the pasta and toss lightly. Season with salt and pepper and eat straight away, this dish won't wait around!

Spaghetti with Clams and Mussels

I ate this for the first time one Christmas in Rome. I returned home certain that it would taste even better made with Irish shellfish – and it did!

Serves 4

50ml (2fl oz) olive oil
3 garlic cloves, crushed
400g (14oz) can chopped
    tomatoes
250ml (9fl oz) white wine
400g (14oz) live mussels
    (see page 44 for
    preparation guidelines)

400g (14oz) fresh clams
    (in shells), scrubbed
500g (1lb 2oz) fresh
    spaghetti
salt and freshly ground
    black pepper

Place a heavy-bottomed saucepan over a medium heat and add the olive oil. When the oil is hot, add the garlic and cook for 2 minutes. Stir in the chopped tomatoes and wine, then cover and cook for 5 minutes.

Season with salt and pepper and add the mussels and clams. Cover the pan and cook for about 8–10 minutes until they have all opened, tossing them in the tomatoes every couple of minutes.

Dump the spaghetti into a big saucepan of boiling salted water and cook for about 3 minutes. Drain and then toss together with the tomato and seafood sauce. Serve straight away.

Soups and Stocks

I love soup. I love the feel-good factor of a hearty broth. I love that soup makes a little go a long way. I love that it's better the day after and the day after that and I love that you can recycle your leftovers and make something great all over again.

The key to a good soup is good stock. It's easy to make and you can go off and do something else while it's cooking. If you've invested in buying organic meat or veg *this* is where you make your money back. You'll get twice, three times the quantity and flavour of stock from organic chickens and veg or the bones from hand-reared beef than you would from intensively farmed or factory-farmed produce. Plus, with a pot of nutritious home-made stock, half your next meal is already prepared. I generally use chicken or vegetable stock in my soups; meat and fish stocks have an intense flavour that is best suited to specific recipes (such as minestrone or bouillabaisse).

Chicken Stock

Making stock is not an exact science. For a basic chicken stock, cover the carcass with cold water, throw in 2 halved onions (I don't even take the skins off), 3 carrots split down the middle, 3 celery sticks and, if you have them, the discarded tops or skins of some peeled leeks. A fresh bouquet garni works well but you can improvise with your own choice of herbs. Season and simmer for up to 1½ hours. Then strain through a sieve and store in a fridge or in a freezer, I find plastic milk bottles are great for storing stock (but don't fill your container right to the top). When you store the stock in the fridge the liquid will turn into a jelly but don't fret! When you are ready to use the stock just tip the jelly into a saucepan over a medium heat and the jelly will immediately turn back to a liquid form.

Vegetable Stock

For a vegetable stock, I throw a chopped carrot, an onion, a few mushrooms, a leek and a bouquet garni into a saucepan, cover with cold water, and bring to the boil. I then reduce the heat and simmer for 1½ hours.

Potato and Wild Garlic Soup

During springtime in Ireland, wild garlic grows in wooded areas.
It has a broad green leaf and produces the most delicate white flowers.
The flavour is more delicate than the garlic bulb.

Serves 6

50g (2 oz) butter
100g (3½ oz) onions,
    roughly chopped
200g (7 oz) potatoes, peeled
    and roughly chopped
300ml (10fl oz) hot stock
    (chicken or vegetable)

bunch of wild garlic leaves
salt and freshly ground
    black pepper
garlic flowers, to garnish

Place a heavy-bottomed saucepan over a medium heat and melt the butter. Add the onions and potatoes and stir well. Cover the pan with a lid and cook for 10 minutes. Add the stock and bring to the boil. Reduce the heat and cook until the potatoes are tender (about 10 minutes).

Transfer to a blender and whizz until the soup has a smooth consistency. Roughly chop up the wild garlic leaves and stir them into the soup. Season with salt and pepper and serve with a sprinkle of wild garlic flowers on top.

Gazpacho

I remember the first time I made this classic cold Spanish soup, it was coming to the end of the day at the market, so I ran around seeing what I could barter off the stall holders. I came home with a huge pile of tomatoes and decided to have a go at making gazpacho. I fed 12 people the next day and sold the rest at the market the following week. It is one of the most delicious soups in the world, cooling yet spicy at the same time – you have to make it!

Serves 8
1kg (2lb 4oz) ripe tomatoes,
   skinned and chopped
2 garlic cloves, crushed
1 red chilli
1 onion, chopped
3 slices white bread
250ml (9fl oz) cold water
2 tbsp olive oil
1 tbsp white wine vinegar
pinch of paprika
salt and freshly ground
   black pepper, to taste

For the garnish:
½ cucumber, diced
2 spring onions (scallions),
   finely chopped

Put all the ingredients (omitting the garnish) in a blender or food processor and process until completely smooth. Transfer to a bowl, cover and leave to chill in the fridge. Serve chilled, garnished with cucumber and spring onion.

Bacon and Cabbage Soup

I love the classic Irish combination of bacon and cabbage. This soup is so comforting that it gives me a taste of home without having to cook a big 'Bacon and Cabbage' dinner.

Serves 6

50g (2oz) butter
100g (3½oz) diced smoked
   streaky bacon, or lardons
120g (4½oz) potatoes,
   peeled and diced
2 garlic cloves, crushed
100g (3½oz) onions,
   chopped

300ml (10fl oz) hot stock
   (chicken or vegetable)
300g (10oz) chopped fresh
   tomatoes
300g (10oz) cabbage,
   shredded
salt and freshly ground
   black pepper

Place a heavy-bottomed saucepan over a medium heat. Add the butter, and when it has melted stir in the smoked bacon, potatoes, garlic and onions. Cover with a lid and cook for 10 minutes.

Add the stock and tomatoes and bring to the boil. Tip in the cabbage, reduce the heat and cook for about 5 minutes until all the vegetables are tender. Season to taste with salt and pepper and serve with buttered chunky bread.

Spiced Pumpkin Soup

I was a trainee chef at Ballymaloe House the first time I saw pumpkin cooked and I admit I had my doubts. I watched head chef Rory O'Connel slide the chopped pumpkin into the oven with just a slurp of olive oil, a sprinkle of sea salt and a handful of fresh rosemary. My first mouthful dispelled any doubt. It had a sweet, pungent taste with a gorgeous creamy texture. I was totally bewitched and spent the rest of the season trying every pumpkin recipe known to mankind.

Serves 8

20g (³/₄oz) butter
1kg (2lb 4oz) pumpkin, deseeded, peeled (if the skin is very tough) and chopped into 2.5cm (1in) pieces
200g (7 oz) onions, chopped
2 garlic cloves, crushed
2 tsp roasted cumin seeds (see page 157)

2 tsp roasted coriander seeds
1.2 litres (2 pints) chicken stock
600ml (1 pint) creamy milk (half cream, half milk)
salt and freshly ground black pepper

Melt the butter in a heavy-bottomed saucepan, then add the pumpkin, onions and garlic. Cover and leave to simmer for about 15 minutes, stirring occasionally. Add the cumin and coriander seeds and sweat for a further 5 minutes.

Stir in the hot chicken stock and creamy milk, and bring to the boil. When the pumpkin is tender, check the seasoning and purée the soup in a blender. Serve hot.

Tip: The peel is perfectly edible, but you should peel it off if it's very tough. Peeling an uncooked pumpkin can be tricky, it's far easier to do this once cooked.

Curried Parsnip and Apple Soup

This is a great autumn soup. At this time of year, you will find an abundance of delicious apples and parsnips at the markets. Why not double the quantities and freeze some for a lazy day?

Serves 4

50g (2oz) butter
1 onion, roughly chopped
1 garlic clove, crushed
2 parsnips, roughly chopped
1 cooking apple, peeled, cored
    and roughly chopped
1 tbsp plain flour
1 tbsp medium curry powder

1 litre (1^3/$_4$ pints) hot stock
    (vegetable or chicken)
100ml (3^1/$_2$ fl oz) double cream
salt and freshly ground
    black pepper
bunch of fresh coriander,
    chopped

Melt the butter in a heavy-bottomed saucepan over a low heat. Stir in the onion, garlic, parsnips and apple, season and then cover the pan and cook for 10 minutes, stirring occasionally. Mix in the flour and curry powder, and keep stirring for 1 minute - this builds up the delicious flavour.

Add the hot stock and cook until the vegetables are tender. Stir in the cream and chopped coriander. Serve hot with crusty white bread.

Darina Allen

Darina Allen is a chef, teacher, author, campaigner, grower, television presenter, and the co-founder of one of the first farmers' markets in Ireland.

The light bulb popped for Darina Allen when, as a young woman, she was in Italy on a cookery course. The teacher proudly presented the class with the finest fare his country had to offer. Darina's heart started thumping because, in that moment, she recognised that Ireland's food was every bit as good as this - as good as any in the world. She just needed to let the world know. Since then she has been a tireless food ambassador for Irish producers.

Darina's belief in healthy, wholesome food, traditional Irish cooking and the excellence of Irish produce all came together in 1983 when she opened Ballymaloe Cooking School at Shanagarry, in County Cork. Ballymaloe, now internationally renowned, teaches traditional Irish cooking but also offers courses as diverse as bee and poultry keeping and smoking your own meat and cheese. In 2005, Darina won the International Association of Culinary Professionals 'Best Cookery Teacher in the World' award. She has written numerous award-winning cookbooks and has had nine television series. She has even cooked breakfast for President Clinton.

As chairperson of Slow Food Ireland she believes passionately in the 'eat local, seasonal and fresh' message. Most of the fruit and vegetables sourced by the Ballymaloe Cookery School and Restaurant are grown in the Ballymaloe organic garden. Organic for Darina is not a luxury but a necessity, if you want to eat nutritious food that is clear of GM and pesticides. She is on the board of the Organic Centre and is also a member of the Consumer Foods and Ingredients Board of An Bord Bia (the promotional body for Irish artisan food producers).

It is for her unstinting support of small producers and championing of the farmers' markets that I salute Darina. She is credited with starting the Midleton Farmers' Markets along with John Potter Cogan and Ted Murphy when, in 1999, John approached Darina because he was worried that the closure of a large food plant in Midleton would leave local farmers with no outlet for their produce. Ted became involved as he is Chairman of the Town Council. Together they came up with a plan for a farmers' market based on ones they had seen in San Francisco, and so Midleton Farmers' Market was born. Ballymaloe Cookery School garden still has a stall there every Saturday selling their own organic fruit and vegetables, eggs, bread, jams and chutneys.

Darina laughs at her own description of herself as 'a free-market anarchist battling for the little man'. The way she sees it she is just doing her bit to safeguard our great traditional food culture.

Darina has been one of my main influences on food in Ireland. Her tireless energy and passion is intoxicating and fuels everyone around her. Without her, I am not sure what would have happened to Irish food.

Darina Allen selling produce from her organic farm at Midleton market.

Darina Allen's Spinach Soup

I first ate this soup when I was on a three-month cookery course at Ballymaloe. Now every time I see spinach at the market I grab it and quickly run home to whizz this up. If you can make a smoothie, you can make this soup – it's that easy.

Serves 6

50g (2 oz) butter
120g (4 ½ oz) potatoes, peeled
   and roughly chopped
100g (3 ½ oz) onions, peeled
   and roughly chopped
600ml (1 pint) stock (chicken
   or vegetable, see page 126)

300g (10 oz) spinach, tough
   stalks removed
salt and freshly ground
   black pepper

Place a heavy-bottomed saucepan over a medium heat and melt the butter. Stir in the potatoes and onions, then cover the pan and reduce the heat to a bare simmer. Sweat for about 15 minutes, stirring occasionally.

Add the hot stock and turn the heat up high. Let the onions and potatoes cook in the stock until they are completely soft, then add the spinach - the spinach will only take 2 minutes to cook.

When the spinach has wilted, pour the mixture into a blender and whizz until the soup has a smooth consistency. Season to taste with salt and pepper and serve hot.

Tips: Variations include adding 1 tablespoon of roughly chopped fresh rosemary when adding the spinach. Alternatively, try adding 1 teaspoon of grated nutmeg when adding the spinach.

Roast Asparagus, Knocklara and Mint Salad

Roasting the asparagus really intensifies and sweetens the flavour as it removes the natural moisture. Knocklara is a beautiful goat's cheese, similar to feta, made by Wolfgang and Agnes Schliebitz in County Waterford.

Serves 4

850g (30 oz) asparagus spears, washed and trimmed

75g (2½ oz) hazelnuts, chopped

6 tbsp extra virgin olive oil

salt and black pepper

juice of 1 lemon

mixed salad leaves (e.g. rocket, cos, frisée or oak's lettuce)

250g (9 oz) Knocklara (or feta), crumbled

Toss the asparagus and chopped hazelnuts in 2 tbsp olive oil. Salt lightly and place on a baking tray. Cook in a preheated oven at 200°C, 400°F, Gas Mark 6 for 12-15 minutes. Remove and cool.

In a mixing bowl, combine the lemon juice, pepper and 4 tablespoons of olive oil. Add the green leaves together with the cooled asparagus and toss gently together. Transfer to a serving dish, sprinkle the cheese over the top and serve.

The Irish Farmers' Market Cookbook

Ballycotton Potato Salad

Willie Scannell is a potato farmer from the fishing village of Ballycotton in East Cork. He grows and sells the famous Ballycotton potatoes at Midleton market. This waxy potato is ideal for this classic dish and marries perfectly with the creamy, thick crème fraîche and zesty lemon.

Serves 4

1kg (2lb 4oz) Ballycotton
    potatoes (or new
    potatoes), washed
salt and freshly ground
    black pepper
300ml (10fl oz) crème fraîche
zest and juice of 2 lemons
bunch of chopped fresh mint

Boil the potatoes in a little salted water until tender. (They should be almost steaming rather than boiling). Drain the potatoes well and slice them in half.

While the potatoes are still warm, add the crème fraîche, lemon zest and juice, and salt and pepper. Stir gently and leave to cool. Add the fresh mint just before serving.

Couscous Salad with Rocket, Knocklara Cheese, Almonds and Apricots

This recipe is so easy to make and is great for parties as it works really well when multiplied. It's also a good lunch box filler.

Serves 2
375g (13oz) couscous
500ml (17½fl oz) boiling water
    (or chicken stock)
50ml (2fl oz) olive oil
2 tbsp flaked almonds
big bunch of fresh rocket
110g (4oz) dried apricots,
    roughly chopped
50g (2oz) Knocklara cheese
    (see page 138) or feta

Put the couscous in a large bowl and pour over the boiling water or chicken stock, if you have it. Cover with a plate and leave the couscous to steam for 10 minutes. When all the liquid has been absorbed, add the olive oil and break the grains up with a fork. Leave to cool.

Heat a frying pan over a low heat and add the almonds. Cook until light brown, tossing all the time as they burn quite easily.

Fold the almonds, rocket, dried apricots and Knocklara cheese into the cooled couscous, and serve.

Gubbeen Farmhouse Warm Salad

Ooohh, creamy runny cheese, crispy bacon and waxy potatoes with fresh green leaves – can it get better? This makes a great lunch dish. If you are unable to get Gubbeen (see pages 76–7), any of your favourite semi-soft cheeses would work well with this recipe, and the same goes for the bacon.

Serves 4

6 tbsp extra virgin olive oil

175g (6oz) smoked Gubbeen bacon lardons

150g (5oz) waxy potatoes, peeled and chopped into large chunks

150g (5oz) Gubbeen cheese (unsmoked), diced

1 tbsp honey

mixed salad leaves (e.g. rocket, cos, mustard leaves, frisée)

50g (2oz) freshly grated Desmond cheese (or Parmesan)

Get your frying pan nice and hot, add 2 tablespoons of olive oil and fry the bacon and potatoes until they are nice and crispy. Turn down the heat to low, add the cheese and honey and the remaining olive oil. Once the cheese begins to get stringy, remove the pan from the heat.

Arrange the salad leaves on 4 serving plates and top with the bacon, potato and cheese mixture. Sprinkle the Desmond cheese over the top.

Beetroot, Goat's Cheese, and Walnut Salad

There is absolutely no comparison between fresh beetroot and the vacuum-packed or canned variety. The former is sweet, succulent and full of flavour while the latter cannot help being anything except bland and anodyne. The difference in taste and texture is such that I would never recommend using beetroot except in season, which, happily, runs from mid-June until the first frosts of winter.

Serves 4

selection of salad leaves
150g (5oz) soft goat's cheese
  (e.g. Ardsallagh, St. Ola, Mine
  Gabhair), cut into wedges
3 cooked beetroots, cut into
  small wedges
10-15 walnuts, coarsely chopped

For the dressing:

1 tbsp balsamic vinegar
3 tbsp extra virgin olive oil
½ tsp Dijon mustard
pinch of sugar

Wash and dry the salad leaves and arrange a small handful of leaves on each serving plate. Divide the goat's cheese and beetroot wedges between the plates.
  Put all the ingredients for the dressing in a small bowl and mix with a spoon. Dress the salad just before serving and sprinkle over the walnuts.

goatscheese
€
20,0 u

Rupert's Mixed Leaves and Flowers with Desmond Shavings and Balsamic Dressing

Rupert Hugh Jones grows a fantastic range of green leaves, as well as heirloom tomatoes and other vegetables, under the name of 'Ballycotton Organics'. He trades throughout the Cork markets. This salad is beautiful as a starter but is also perfect for accompanying any dish, whether a hearty fish pie or light pasta dish.

Serves 2
3 tbsp balsamic vinegar
1 tbsp extra virgin olive oil
1 tsp Dijon mustard
mixed salad leaves, nasturtiums
   and dandelion flowers
80g (3oz) Desmond cheese
   (or Parmesan)

To make the dressing, mix the balsamic vinegar, olive oil and mustard in a small bowl.
   Place the salad leaves and flowers on serving plates. Shave the Desmond cheese over the top and dress with the balsamic dressing just before serving.

Wild Mushrooms with Rocket and Desmond Cheese

Simple yet so tasty. This recipe is all about the quality of the ingredients.

Serves 2
50ml (2fl oz) olive oil
500g 91lb 2oz) wild
    mushrooms (e.g. shiitake,
    oyster, ceps)
juice of 1 lemon
salt and freshly ground
    black pepper
100g (3½oz) Desmond
    cheese (or Parmesan)
1 large bunch of fresh rocket

Place a frying pan over a high heat and add the olive oil. When the oil starts to smoke, throw in the wild mushrooms and lemon juice and cook evenly - this takes about 5 minutes. Season with salt and lots of freshly ground pepper (mushrooms love pepper).

    Transfer the mushrooms to a serving dish and leave to cool. When cool, shave the Desmond cheese over them - a vegetable peeler is great for this - and fold in the fresh rocket.

Courgette and Lemon Salad

Every year there is a glut of courgettes at the market. This is a very simple but really delicious way to use them up. I particularly love eating this salad with roast chicken.

Serves 4
3 medium courgettes
juice of 1 lemon
50ml (2fl oz) extra virgin
   olive oil
salt and freshly ground
   black pepper

Slice the courgettes very thinly, using a mandolin if you have one. Place a saucepan of water over a high heat, and when the water comes to the boil, drop in the courgettes and cook for about 1 minute (just to blanch them). Drain in a colander and wrap them in a clean tea towel to dry them off.

Arrange them on a serving dish, pour over a drizzle of olive oil and the lemon juice, and season with salt and pepper. Leave to marinate for about 30 minutes before serving.

Pestos & Dips

Tasty Sauces

Forget mayo, ketchup and mustard – today, the farmers' market stalls are heaving with salsas, seasonal pesto, dips and tapenades. I think this explosion of interest in condiments is influenced by people travelling more, being inspired by food abroad and bringing new ideas home. Also, the great variety of ingredients, spices and fresh herbs available encourage people to experiment with bold fusions of flavours. I am delighted to see old skills and recipes being passed on and used as a starting point for new recipes. It is also a constantly changing market as each season produces a fresh new selection of ingredients to work with: lovely spicy aubergine dips in the autumn, fresh pesto in spring and zingy salsas and fruity barbecue sauces in summer.

These are just a few producers you will catch at the markets: Sonia Bower's 'Inner Pickle'; Laragh Stuart's 'Laragh Foods'; 'The Real Olive Company' (see page 154); 'Saucy Sauces' and 'Just Organic'.

Summer Basil Pesto

Home-made basil pesto is incredibly versatile and greatly improves the taste and appearance of any number of dishes. It goes well with pasta, chicken or fish. Best of all, it takes only a few minutes to make and will keep in the fridge for up to three weeks. If basil is not available, you can use parsley, coriander, wild garlic or rocket instead.

Makes approx. 200ml (7fl oz)

110g (4oz) fresh basil leaves
150ml (5fl oz) extra virgin olive oil
25g (1oz) pine kernels
2 garlic cloves, peeled

50g (2oz) freshly grated
   Desmond cheese
   (or Parmesan)
salt and pepper

Put the basil, olive oil, pine kernels, garlic and grated cheese in a food processor and blend for a couple of minutes. Season to taste and that's it!

Coriander and Goat's Cheese Pesto

Fiona Burke, who has a fabulous farmhouse cheese stall at Midleton farmers' market, used to make this to sell when there was a glut of coriander. This is my own version, which is delicious with tagliatelle.

Makes approx. 200ml (7fl oz)

150g (5oz) fresh coriander
150ml (5fl oz) extra virgin olive oil
25g (1oz) pine kernels
50g (2oz) soft goat's cheese

50g (2oz) freshly grated
   Desmond cheese
   (or Parmesan)
pinch of salt

Put all the ingredients into a food processor and whizz together until well blended.

Sun-dried Tomato Pesto

This pesto is fantastic with frittata, drizzled over a goat's cheese bruschetta, or folded through fresh pasta.

Makes 150ml (5fl oz)

100g (3 1/2 oz) sun-dried tomatoes
2 garlic cloves, peeled
75g (2 1/2 oz) freshly grated
    Desmond cheese (or Parmesan)

30g (1 oz) pine nuts
100ml (3 1/2 fl oz) extra virgin
    olive oil

Put all the ingredients into a food processor and blend for 10 seconds. Store in the fridge until required – it will keep for up to 1 month.

Tapenade

In the markets in Ireland you may come across a stall called 'The Real Olive Company', which is owned and run by Toby Simmonds and Jenny Rose Clarke. They import a fantastic range of olives, sun-dried tomatoes, oil and vinegars. When I first became involved in the markets, I was against imported goods, but I now feel that if we are unable to grow or produce something ourselves, we can be a bit more relaxed. The greater the selection you have, the more successful the market will be, and that benefits the local farmer.

Makes approx. 80g (3oz)

5 tbsp olive oil
70g (2 1/2 oz) black Kalamata
    olives, pitted

salt and freshly ground
    black pepper
2 garlic cloves, chopped

Place all the ingredients in a blender and whizz until you get a smooth consistency. This is delicious with crunchy toast, rocket and Parmesan.

Guacamole

It is often the way that the most impressive looking items on a menu are the quickest and easiest to make. For proof of this, look no further than this traditional Mexican dip. It takes no more than 5 minutes to create and can also be used as a sandwich filler or served with grilled chicken, or even as a topping for bruschetta with goat's cheese.

Makes 2

1 ripe avocado
1 garlic clove, crushed
1–2 tbsp freshly squeezed lime
    or lemon juice
1 tbsp extra virgin olive oil
1 tbsp chopped fresh coriander
salt and freshly ground
    black pepper

Cut the avocado in half, discard the stone and scoop out the flesh. Mash with a fork, then add the garlic, lime or lemon juice, olive oil and coriander. Season to taste with salt and pepper. Cover with cling film immediately as it discolours very fast.

Tip: To keep your guacamole nice and green, place the avocado stone on top of the dip and cover with cling film.

The Irish Farmers' Market Cookbook

Cool Cucumber and Yogurt Dip

The essence of this recipe is good yogurt, and there are many delicious Irish varieties: Glenilen, Glenisk and Knockatee to name a few.

Makes approx. 250ml (9fl oz)

½ medium-sized cucumber
½ tsp whole cumin seeds

150ml (5fl oz) natural yogurt
1 tbsp chopped fresh coriander

Chop the cucumber into small dice – about 5mm (¼in). Roast the cumin seeds in a preheated oven at 180°C, 350°F, Gas Mark 4 for 5 minutes, or you can dry-fry them in a pan for about 3 minutes or until you can smell their aroma. Mix together the cumin, yogurt, cucumber and fresh coriander in a bowl.

Roasted Aubergine Dip

Creamy and spicy, this aubergine dip is similar to the Middle Eastern dish baba ghanoush. It is fantastic served with toasted pitta bread.

Makes approx. 150ml (5fl oz)

1 large aubergine
50ml (2fl oz) olive oil
1 tsp cumin seeds
1 garlic clove, peeled

50g (2 oz) freshly grated Parmesan
  cheese
4 black olives, pitted
salt and freshly grated black pepper

Place the aubergine in a roasting pan and drizzle some olive oil on top. Use your hands to coat it in the oil. Cook in a preheated oven at 180°C, 350°F, Gas Mark 4 for 20 minutes, then remove and set aside to cool. Chop into large chunks.

In a frying pan, dry-roast the cumin for 2 minutes or until you can smell the aroma from the spice. Place the aubergine, garlic, grated Parmesan, olives, cumin seeds and a splash of olive oil in a blender, and blend to a smooth consistency. Season with salt and pepper.

Roasted Red Pepper Hummus

Hummus is dangerous for me as I could eat kilos of it! If you don't have peppers to hand, just omit them for a plain hummus.

Makes approx. 500g (1lb 2oz)
1 red pepper
60ml (2fl oz) olive oil
2 garlic cloves, peeled
420g (15oz) cooked, canned
    chickpeas
juice of 1 lemon
salt and freshly ground
    black pepper

Rub the red pepper with a little of the olive oil and place in a roasting pan. Cook in a preheated oven at 180°C, 350°F, Gas Mark 4 for 20 minutes.

Remove and place in a bowl. Cover with cling film or a plate to create steam and help loosen the skin, and leave for 2 minutes. Peel off the skin, cut the pepper in half and remove the seeds.

Place the garlic and roasted red pepper in a food processor and whizz until finely chopped. Add the chickpeas and process until well blended. Then add the lemon juice and drizzle in the remaining olive oil through the feed tube to make a fairly coarse paste. Season to taste and spoon into a serving bowl.

Rachel McCormac's Sicilian Hummus

The very talented Rachel McCormac and Jenny Rose Clarke run the wonderful 'Sandwich Stall' in the Old English Market. This recipe is inspired by the almond-flavoured hummus Rachel tasted while on holiday in Sicily.

Makes approx. 700g (1lb 9oz)

500g (1lb 2oz) cooked, canned chickpeas
30g (1oz) pine nuts
30g (1oz) salted almonds
juice of 1 lemon
2 garlic cloves, peeled
bunch of fresh basil
50ml (2 fl oz) olive oil
sea salt

Put all the ingredients into a food processor and blend well. Add a splash of water – just enough to get a smooth consistency. This is delicious served with toasted pitta bread.

Summer Tomato and Coriander Salsa

This is another brilliantly versatile condiment.

Serves 4

4 ripe tomatoes, chopped
1 red onion, chopped
1 red chilli, finely chopped
2 tbsp chopped fresh coriander
pinch of sugar
sea salt and freshly ground black pepper

Mix all the ingredients together in a bowl. Season to taste with salt and pepper.

Cheese

The Cheese Revolution

At the forefront of the Irish food revolution that started in the 1970s were the artisan cheese makers. At that time, cheese making, once a great Irish tradition, had all but died out. But a small group of pioneering cheese makers including Giana Ferguson, Bill Hogan, Breda Maher, Jeffa Gill, and Norman and Veronica Steele, revived the tradition. They were a great success, exporting their cheeses to the UK and America, attracting food writers and chefs from all over the world and winning prizes internationally.

Cheese reflects the land it has come from more than any other food product. In Ireland, we have a mild maritime climate that allows cattle to graze all year round on fields carpeted with a broad range of grasses and heather, which give the milk a richness and intensity. The producers received support from farmers' markets and chefs keen to put their cheeses on restaurant menus; as well as from delis and upmarket supermarkets. In London, Randolph Hodgson of Neal's Yard is a huge supporter and supplier of Irish artisan cheese, and in Ireland we have the Sheridan cheesemongers. And of course there was, and is, the exceptional quality and variety of the cheeses themselves. For example:

- Mount Callan – made using the traditional Cheddar method, pressed and bound in cheesecloth, and naturally matured on wood.
- Durrus – a rind-washed, sweet, fragrant, nutty cheese of real character.
- Cooleeney – a Camembert-style soft cheese with a distinct mushroomy aroma and a rich, semi-liquid interior.
- Bellingham Blue – a semi-hard, natural rind cheese.
- Desmond – hard with a quick impact and a sharp resonant aftertaste; try using it as an alternative to Parmesan.

The variety of flavours, textures and types of cheese is staggering when you think that between 1840 and 1970 the tradition of cheese making had nearly disappeared.

You would think the government would be bending over backwards to promote and help the raw milk cheese producers. Instead, they are stringently interpreting outdated and inappropriate EU regulations which may force cheese makers to use pasteurised milk instead of raw milk or risk going out of business. The problem with pasteurised milk is that it kills the micro floras that give great cheese that exceptional taste and uniqueness. Jeffa Gill, who makes the Durrus farmhouse cheese, is a coordinator of the Slow Food Irish Raw Cow's Milk Cheese Presidium. For Jeffa, the conservation of raw milk cheese production is important for many reasons, but primarily, 'for taste, for tradition and for best practice cheese making'. Bill Hogan, who produces Desmond cheese, is determined to resist pasteurisation because 'the flavour and integrity of the cheese would suffer'.

We need to protect and support our raw milk cheeses because: they are unique and individual, hand-crafted, and organically developed by the producer with real passion (something you can't reproduce on an industrial scale); because raw milk producers can respond to the cheese during the process intuitively and flexibly; because it is part of our tradition, our story; but above and beyond all, because these raw milk cheeses are so good.

The Irish Farmers' Market Cookbook

Giana Ferguson's Baked Cheese with Winter Herbs

Gooey, warm and delicious. This is quick to prepare and quicker to devour!

Serves 2
1 baby Gubbeen (approximately
    470g/1lb) or your favourite
    whole semi-soft cheese
1 tbsp chopped mixed fresh herbs
    (e.g. thyme and rosemary)
2 garlic cloves, chopped
freshly ground black pepper

Cut the cheese in half horizontally to make 2 rounds. Sprinkle the herbs, garlic and black pepper on the bottom half and replace the top. Place on a large piece of kitchen foil and wrap the foil up around the cheese, forming a steam vent on top with the excess foil. This will let out the moisture while the cheese bakes.

Place the cheese on a baking sheet and bake in a preheated oven at 170°C, 325°F, Gas Mark 3 for 20 minutes or until the cheese is soft and runny. Spread on slices of chunky bread while the cheese is still warm.

The Durrus Melt Down!

This recipe was given to me by the pioneering cheese maker Jeffa Gill, who makes the award-winning Durrus cheese at her farm in West Cork.

Serves 6

900g (2lb) waxy potatoes, peeled and cubed
2 tbsp olive oil
2 onions, diced
200g (7oz) bacon rashers, cut into small pieces

400g (14oz) or 1 small Durrus (or a semi-soft cheese of your choice), cut into cubes with the rind removed
250ml (9fl oz) crème fraîche
salt and freshly ground black pepper

Steam or parboil the potatoes for 10-15 minutes, depending on size. They should be al dente. Meanwhile, place a saucepan over a medium heat and add the olive oil. Add the onions, cover with a lid and cook until soft. Remove the lid and add the bacon and fry for a further 5-7 minutes.

Put all the ingredients in a greased shallow ovenproof dish, and mix gently. Bake in a preheated oven at 180°C, 350°F, Gas Mark 4 for 15-20 minutes. Stir gently halfway through cooking.

Serve with a green salad, and a cracking bottle of wine of your choice - it is equally good with red or white.

Bellingham Blue Bruschetta with Caramelised Pears

This wonderful pungent, creamy cheese with a semi-hard, natural rind has won a number of international accolades, including Gold Medal at the prestigious British Cheese awards.

Serves 4

2 pears
a knob of butter
2 tbsp honey
8 slices sourdough bread
(see page 27)
1 tbsp extra virgin olive oil

150g (5oz) Bellingham Blue
cheese, or any blue
cheese
salt and freshly ground
black pepper
1 handful of walnuts,
roughly chopped

Peel, quarter, core and thinly slice the pears. Heat a frying pan over a high heat and add the butter. Tip in the pear slices and add the honey, then reduce the heat and fry gently until caramelised, turning frequently.

Meanwhile, toast the sourdough bread. Sprinkle the toast with olive oil, and crumble the cheese on top. Pop under a hot grill and grill until the cheese begins to melt. Transfer the toast to a warm plate and scatter over the caramelised pears. Season with salt and pepper and sprinkle with the walnuts.

Raw Milk Cheese Frittata with Sun-dried Tomato Pesto

This is a great standby recipe when you haven't got much food in the house.

Serves 4
6 eggs
salt and freshly ground black pepper
a knob of butter
100g (3½ oz) cooked potato, diced
50g (2 oz) Durrus cheese or your
    favourite semi-soft cheese
shavings of Desmond cheese
    (or Parmesan)

Beat the eggs together and season with salt and pepper. Melt the butter in a small, ovenproof frying pan or omelette pan, tilting the pan to coat it evenly. Add the eggs to the pan and turn down the heat as low as it will go. Add the potato and both cheeses. Leave to cook gently for 2 minutes – the underneath should be set and the top still runny.

Then, place the pan under a preheated hot grill until the top sets. Slide a knife under the frittata and tip out gently on to a plate. Drizzle some pesto on top (see page 154). Serve sliced into wedges.

Sheridans

Revolutions don't happen all by themselves. So what were the seeds that fuelled Ireland's gastronomic revolution? We had the natural resources, surrounded by sea, fast-flowing fresh water rivers and rich, fertile farm land; we had the heroic producers with the imagination and determination to succeed; we had the farmers' markets as a point of sale for the artisan producer; and we had the support of organisations and individuals who were determined to promote the produce.

Left to right: Seamus Sheridan, Kevin Sheridan and Fiona Corbett.

No-one has done more to promote Irish cheese and artisan foods in the last ten years than the Sheridan brothers, Seamus and Kevin. They were early supporters of the farmers' markets and were always champions of Irish cheeses. In 1995, they set up a stall in the Galway market selling Irish farmhouse cheese. The stall was a roaring success, which led them to open their first shop, Sheridan's Cheesemongers in Galway, where the cheeses were piled floor to ceiling. You'd find all the great iconic cheese there: Milleens, Durrus, Gubbeen, Ardrahan, Cashel Blue, Desmond and many more besides, because the brothers were, and still are, unstinting in their quest to source great Irish cheese. The shop moved a few years later to its current location, and houses a kitchen for the production of Sheridan's own terrines, pestos and other home-made delicacies.

The Irish cheeses were joined by their European farmhouse cousins, as well as olive oils, cured meats, honeys and many other artisan foods that weren't traditionally made in Ireland. In 1997, Seamus and Kevin were joined by a third partner, Fiona Corbett. Together they quickly opened two more shops in Galway and Dublin, including the new 'Wine Shop Upstairs', selling a wider range of artisan products.

Their business continues to thrive and grow along with their boundless enthusiasm for, and pride in, the produce. I never leave one of their shops without being given a taste of a new cheese - 'C'mere Clodagh, you have to try this' - a slice of newly sourced ham, or some other delicacy fresh into the shop. And their commitment and energy doesn't stop there. Seamus, Fiona and Kevin still run stalls in markets throughout Dublin and Galway. The Sheridans are tireless promoters of Irish cheese abroad, exporting cheeses all over Europe; and they supply their products to markets, restaurants and shops throughout the country. They also play a seminal role in Slow Food Ireland.

For me, the Sheridans aren't just a big part of the Irish food revolution, they embody its spirit. They are passionate, determined, and talented and, let's face it, more than just a bit cool.

Kevin Sheridan passes me some cheese to taste – it was gorgeous!

Ardsallagh Cheese Wrapped in Roasted Red Peppers

This is a lovely, simple recipe using this delicious soft goat's cheese, made by Jane and Gerard Murphy and sold throughout the farmers' markets in Cork and Dublin.

Serves 2 for starters or
4 for canapés
4 tbsp olive oil
1 red pepper
2 tbsp flaked almonds
70g (2 ½ oz) Ardsallagh
    goat's cheese
a bunch of fresh rocket leaves
salt and freshly ground
    black pepper

Drizzle 2 tablespoons of olive oil over the red pepper and place in a preheated hot oven at 200°C, 400°F, Gas Mark 6 for about 15 minutes until the pepper is soft.

While the pepper is roasting, lightly toast the flaked almonds in a frying pan.

Remove the peppers from the oven, place in a bowl and cover with cling film. Leave for 5 minutes to loosen the skin and then peel it off and remove the seeds inside. Slice the flesh into 5cm (2in) strips.

With a dessertspoon, scoop out a little soft goat's cheese, roll in the toasted almonds and season with salt and pepper. Place the goat's cheese on the roasted red pepper and a couple of rocket leaves and wrap. Continue and place all the stuffed peppers on a serving dish and drizzle over 2 tablespoons of olive oil.

Desmond Cheese Roasted Potatoes

Desmond cheese is made by Bill Hogan in Schull, West Cork. It is a hard raw-milk cheese, with a fabulous strong flavour. If you are unable to get your hands on this fabulous cheese, Parmesan makes a good substitute.

Makes 6 roasted potatoes
6 medium roasting potatoes
3 tbsp butter, melted
salt and lemon-pepper
150g (5oz) Desmond cheese,
    grated (or Parmesan)
2 tbsp dry breadcrumbs

Either peel the potatoes or scrub them well. Make small slices along each potato, about three-quarters of the way through it - if the potato is placed in a large spoon the edges of the spoon will prevent you from slicing right through it. Place the potatoes in a greased baking dish and brush each one with melted butter before sprinkling with salt and lemon-pepper.

Bake in a preheated oven at 220°C, 425°F, Gas Mark 7 for 45 minutes. Remove from the oven and sprinkle with grated Desmond cheese and breadcrumbs. Return to the oven and continue baking for 15 minutes or until the potatoes are tender and the crust is slightly browned.

Preserving

Jams, Pickles and Chutneys

Preserving is as old an art as wall painting. Humans have long found a way to make food last: using fruit or vegetables from one season and adding oil, vinegar, lemon or sugar to store it through the next. It is messy and it does take over the kitchen, but home-made tastes so much better – and it's really quite easy. With home-made pickles, chutneys and jam you can taste real pieces of fruit or vegetables and actually appreciate their flavour, not just the sugar or vinegar. Don't underestimate the feel-good factor. That feeling of self sufficiency, of providing, the satisfaction of cooking up the ingredients, bottling them in lovely jars and hand-labelling them; it's a maximum sense of achievement for a very simple task with the best pay-off – you get to eat it!

Notes for Preserving
- A lot of sugar is used in preserving but you can substitute honey if you wish. Add half the quantity that you would of sugar.
- Stainless steel pots are the best for cooking preserves.
- Sterilise your clean jars by placing them in a hot oven for about an hour.

Summer Cucumber Pickle

I used to sell this pickle at the market – it is fantastic with pâtés, cold meats and poached fish, and it lasts for a couple of weeks in the fridge.

Makes approx. 400ml (14fl oz)

1 cucumber

1 onion, peeled

80g (3oz) white granulated sugar

250ml (9fl oz) cider vinegar

1 tsp salt

Using a mandolin or sharp knife, thinly slice the cucumber and onion into a large bowl. Then pour the sugar, vinegar and salt over the cucumber and onion. Cover with a towel and leave for about 2 hours.

Give the cucumber pickle a good stir and leave for 1 hour. Either store in an airtight container or screw top jar in the fridge or bottle in a sterilised jar. Will last for up to a month.

Autumn Pickled Courgettes

This is a great combination of mild courgettes and zingy mustard seeds. Like the cucumber pickle, it goes well with pâtés and cold meats.

Makes approx. 500ml (17½fl oz)

2 courgettes, about 20cm (8in) long

1 onion, peeled

150g (5oz) granuated sugar

250ml (9fl oz) cider vinegar

2 tsp yellow mustard seeds

1 tsp salt

Cut the courgettes in half widthways and, using a mandolin (or sharp knife), thinly slice them lengthways and place in a bowl. Thinly slice the onion in the same way and mix with the courgettes.

Pour the sugar, vinegar, mustard seeds and salt over the courgettes and onion. Cover with a tea towel and set aside for about 2 hours. Give the pickle a good stir and leave for 1 more hour. Either store covered in a fridge or bottled in a sterilised jar. It will last for up to a month.

Mrs G's Gooseberry Jam

Helen Gee is the queen of jam-making at the farmers' markets.

Makes approx. 12 x 250ml (9fl oz) jars

2.5kg (5½ lb) gooseberries, topped and tailed

2.5kg (5½ lb) white granulated sugar

1.2 litres (2 pints) water

2 heads of elderflowers

Put the gooseberries and sugar in a clean bowl and pour over the water. Leave to steep overnight.

The next day, rinse the elderflower heads in cold water and shake dry. Cut off the flowers with scissors, put them in a muslin bag and tie securely.

Transfer the gooseberries in their sugary water to a large saucepan together with the elderflowers. Stir gently over a low heat until the sugar dissolves and the gooseberries are soft. Turn up the heat to high and boil rapidly until setting point is reached – about 15 minutes. Test it by spooning a little of the jam onto a cold saucer and pushing it with a spoon. If the jam wrinkles, it is set.

Remove the pan from the heat and skim the film off the top of the jam. Cool a little and then transfer to sterilised jars. Cover, label and date. The jam will keep for up to 6 months, stored in a cool, dry place.

Autumn Spiced Apple Chutney

I used to sell this chutney at the markets in pretty kilner jars. It's so good with pâté, cheese, sausages and also mixed in with a potato stuffing for game or pork. It will keep for up to 6 months in a cool place.

Makes 12 x 220ml (8fl oz) jars

2kg (5lb) cooking apples, (e.g. Bramleys), peeled, cored and chopped
450g (1lb) brown sugar
2 onions, finely chopped
4 tsp turmeric
approx. 20 cloves

500ml (17½ fl oz) cider vinegar
2 tsp chilli powder
2 tsp salt
2 tsp black pepper
10cm (4 in) piece fresh root ginger, peeled and finely chopped

Place the apples in a heavy-bottomed saucepan. Stir in all the other ingredients, then cover the pan and bring to the boil.

Reduce the heat to low and give the chutney a stir. Be careful that the chutney doesn't stick to the bottom of the pan – if it has already, remove from the heat, cover with a lid and leave for about 15 minutes before stirring again. Cook, uncovered, for about 1 hour, stirring regularly, until reduced and thickened.

Leave to cool completely, then transfer the chutney to sterilised jars and label. It will last for up to 6 months but is at its best after 1 month.

Tips:
- If you don't have chilli powder use 1 red chilli, deseeded.
- The easiest way to peel ginger is to use the tip of a teaspoon to scrape off the skin.
- You can also add 150g (5oz) raisins. Add in at the same time as the apples.

Rhubarb Chutney

Makes 3 x 250ml (9fl oz) jars

375g (12oz) rhubarb, trimmed
and diced
1 cooking apple, peeled and
chopped
80g (3oz) brown sugar
125ml (4½ fl oz) cider vinegar

150g (5oz) raisins
1 tbsp lemon juice
1 tsp fresh root ginger, peeled
and grated
½ tsp ground cumin

Combine all the ingredients in a heavy-bottomed saucepan. Bring slowly to the boil, then reduce the heat and simmer for about 10 minutes or until the rhubarb and apple are very soft but still hold their shape. Do not allow them to turn into mush. Adjust the seasoning to taste.

Now cool the chutney and transfer to an airtight container to keep it fresh. It will keep for 1 week in the refrigerator. To store for a longer time or to present as a gift, pack it into sterilised jars.

Farmers' Market Summer Chutney

Makes 6 x 220ml (8fl oz) jars

1 green cabbage
3 onions, peeled
500g (1lb 2oz) ripe tomatoes
4 red or green peppers,
quartered and deseeded
750ml (1¼ pints) white
wine vinegar

1 tbsp salt
320g (12oz) brown sugar
1 cinnamon stick
5 cloves
1 tsp black mustard seeds
½ tsp cayenne pepper

Chop the cabbage, onions, tomatoes and peppers into 2.5cm (1in) cubes and place in a heavy-bottomed saucepan. Add in the remaining ingredients, cover and cook over a medium heat for about 15 minutes. Then remove the lid, reduce the heat and leave to cook for a further 20 minutes.

Leave to cool completely, then transfer to sterilised jars and label. This chutney will last for up to 6 months.

Summer Berry Jam

This is like a burst of summer! My favourite way to eat summer berry jam is with a hot scone and some whipped cream...

Makes approx. 6 x 250ml (9fl oz) jars

1kg (2lb 4oz) summer berries
    (e.g. raspberries, strawberries,
    blackberries, redcurrants,
    loganberries)
1kg (2lb 4oz) white granulated
    sugar

Place all the berries in a heavy-bottomed saucepan over a low heat and leave to simmer for about 15 minutes. Add the sugar and keep stirring until it all dissolves.

Turn up the heat and bring to the boil. Leave to boil until the jam begins to set (see page 178).

Pour the hot jam into sterilised jars and leave to cool. Cover with a disc of greaseproof or waxed paper and a lid. Store in a cool, dry place for up to 3 months.

Blackberry and Apple Jam

Makes approx. 6 x 250ml (9fl oz) jars

500g (1lb 2oz) cooking apples, peeled, cored and roughly chopped

250ml (9fl oz) water
500g (1lb 2oz) blackberries
rind of 1 lemon, grated
1kg (2lb 4oz) white granulated sugar

Place the apples in a heavy-bottomed saucepan with the water. Cover and simmer over a low heat for 10 minutes. Add the blackberries and lemon rind and then stir in the sugar, continuing to stir until it has dissolved.

Bring to the boil and keep boiling until the jam begins to set (see page 178). Pour the hot jam into sterilised jars and leave to cool, then cover with a disc of greaseproof paper or a waxed paper disc and a lid. Store in a cool, dry place for up to 3 months.

Semi Sun-dried Tomatoes

It is great having a stock of these as tomatoes don't keep for very long and they are delicious in everything from salads to sandwiches.

Makes 24
6 tomatoes (ripe but not too soft)
2 tbsp salt
150ml (5fl oz) extra virgin olive oil
1 sprig fresh rosemary and 1 garlic
    clove (optional)

Cut the tomatoes into quarters and scoop out the seeds and juice. Sprinkle salt over the tomatoes and place on a cooling rack. If you have a sunny conservatory, you can leave them there for 3–4 days, uncovered, or you can place them on the lowest heat possible in the oven for 2–3 hours.

Place the dried tomatoes in a sterilised jar and cover with olive oil. I like to add a sprig of rosemary and a clove of garlic for flavour. They will keep for about 3 weeks.

Preserved Lemons

These lemons are delicious chopped up in a couscous salad or roasted with a chicken.

Makes 20 preserved lemons wedges

10 unwaxed lemons

salt

10 peppercorns

10 coriander seeds

4 bay leaves

5 cloves

1 cinnamon stick

Cut 5 of the lemons into quarters and remove the pips. Sprinkle 1 teaspoon of salt into a sterilised jar and then press a layer of lemon quarters on top. Cover with 2 teaspoons of salt, a couple of peppercorns and coriander seeds, a bay leaf and a clove. Repeat this process until you reach the top of the jar.

Break the cinnamon stick in half and push it down the side of the jar. Juice the remaining 5 lemons and pour the juice into the jar. Seal and place in a dark, cool place for 3 weeks before using.

Home-made Lemonade with Lemon Balm

Makes approx. 600ml (1 pint) lemonade syrup

4 lemons

2 oranges

1.5 litres (2½ pints) water

For the stock syrup:

450g (1lb) white granulated sugar

600ml (1 pint) water

5 lemon balm leaves

To make the stock syrup, dissolve the sugar in the water over a gentle heat, stirring well. Add the lemon balm leaves and bring to the boil. Boil for 2 minutes and then leave to cool.

Juice the lemons and oranges and mix well with 450ml (¾ pint) of the cooled stock syrup. Add water to taste.

Desserts, Baking
& Chocolate

Home Baking

Home baking was something my mother's generation took for granted. Women baked on certain days and would usually make scones, tea bread and something a bit fancy to see the family through the week. I remember baking-day treats, like being allowed to lick the bowl, or make dough men or heart shapes from pastry off-cuts if my mother was making a pie. In those days every girl left school knowing how to make shortcrust pastry, scones, sponges and crumbles.

The hectic pace at which we live our lives today means men and women rarely have time to bake at home, but the yearning for a fresh buttermilk scone with jam and clotted cream or a buttery sponge that melts in your mouth is a strong one. Luckily, at the farmers' markets we have a host of excellent bakers selling hand-baked goods that fill the gap for us.

So why are artisan bakers' cakes and breads so much better than the mass-produced cakes? What the big manufacturers put in (preservatives, flavourings, colourings, artificial sweeteners, stabilisers, modified starches, and all the additives used to keep costs down and to prolong shelf life) are exactly what the artisan baker leaves out.

Artisan bakers source the best ingredients, from butter and sugar to fruit and nuts. Their products will be freshly baked, usually on the day, and they have those 'secret' ingredients the big producers can never copy: passion and pride.

Richard Graham Leigh, who owns RGL Patisserie in Dunmanway, is a perfect example. He used to work in London, brightening the lives of city bankers and stockbrokers with his exquisite high teas. When he retired he and his wife, Jane, moved to West Cork. His interest in good food led him to Clontakilty Farmers' Market. I met Richard around this time - he was getting involved in the markets and inevitably set up his own stall selling freshly baked cakes. I used to collect cakes from Richard at the crack of dawn to sell at other markets: the most fantastic frangipanes, almond pastry creams quite different from marzipan, pecan fingers, brioche, cookies, lemon bars - *mmmmm*. Unsurprisingly, Richard was a huge success. Now he and Jane have a commercial bakery next to the house and continue making cakes in the finest tradition using only the best ingredients available. He supplies over ten shops and restaurants and my cousin, Barrie Tyner, still sells his patisseries through Midleton and Ennis farmers' markets - another grand tradition I'm pleased to see being upheld.

Baked Cashel Blue Cheesecake with Apricots

I'll be honest - it takes some time to prepare but for a special occasion it really is worth the effort.

Serves 8
200g (7oz) Cashel Blue
    cheese
400g (14oz) mascarpone
50ml (2fl oz) water
500g (1lb 2oz) caster sugar
6 eggs, separated
80g (3oz) cornflour (sieved)
pinch of salt

For the apricots:
450g (1lb) caster sugar
600ml (1 pint) water
8 apricots, halved and
    stoned

Line a 23cm (9in) spring-form baking tin with baking paper. In a large bowl, mix the two cheeses together. Put the sugar and the water in a saucepan and bring to the boil, stirring until dissolved.

In a clean bowl, beat the egg yolks with a whisk until light and fluffy, add the sugar solution and cornflour and continue to beat until the mixture has cooled, then fold in the cheese mixture. Set aside to cool.

In a clean, dry bowl, whisk the egg whites and salt until they form stiff peaks. Carefully fold the egg whites into the cheese mixture using a metal spoon or spatula (this helps prevent the air being knocked out) until well amalgamated. Pour the mixture into the lined baking tin.

Meanwhile, poach the apricots. Dissolve the sugar in the water over a medium heat, stirring until the sugar dissolves, then add the apricots and cook for appoximately 15 minutes or until the apricots are tender.

Bake in a preheated oven at 170°C, 325°F, Gas Mark 3 for 25-30 minutes. Leave to cool and serve with the poached apricots.

Dad's Amazing Baked Apples

When I was growing up, my dad would come home during his lunch break to prepare a three-course dinner for us, which would be served at 6pm on the dot! With a meagre budget, he experimented with every type of apple dessert, but this was my favourite. He still makes this when I go home for a visit!

Serves 4
4 cooking apples
100g (3½ oz) brown sugar
2 tsp runny honey
2 tsp ground cinnamon
15g (½ oz) butter
16 cloves
whipped cream, to serve

Remove the cores of the apples with an apple corer. With a teaspoon, enlarge the cavity to double its size. Fill each apple with the brown sugar, honey and cinnamon, and place a small knob of butter on top. Pierce each apple with 4 cloves.

Place the apples in a baking dish and cook in a preheated oven at 180°C, 350°F, Gas Mark 4 for 30 minutes. Serve hot with whipped cream.

Tip: You can also fill the apples with different types of dried fruit or nuts, such as apricots, raisins, prunes, hazelnuts or nibbed almonds. Just roughly chop and mix them in with the sugar.

Apple and Hazelnut Crumble

Many of our wonderful old Irish apple varieties are dying out due to the influx of foreign varieties. So, the next time you're tempted, take a bite out of something local – seek out Irish apples at the farmers' markets and be reminded of just how good a native apple can taste.

Serves 6
500g (1lb 2oz) cooking
    apples, peeled, cored
    and chopped rough
    into chunks
60g (2oz) white granulated
    sugar
1 tbsp water

For the crumble:
60g (2oz) butter
150g (5oz) plain white flour
50g (2oz) hazelnuts, roughly
    chopped

First, make the filling. Put the apples, sugar and water in a saucepan and simmer until the apples just begin to break down (you don't want to end up with mush). Remove from the heat and leave to cool.

Meanwhile, make the crumble. In a large bowl, rub the butter into the flour until is resembles breadcrumbs. Be careful not to rub the mixture too fine as you won't get a crunchy finish to the crumble, it is the butter that creates the crunch. Mix in the hazelnuts.

Spoon the filling into an ovenproof dish and sprinkle the crumble mixture on top. Cook in a preheated oven at 200°C, 400°F, Gas mark 6 for 30 minutes or until the crumble is cooked and golden. This is delicious served with Glenilen clotted cream.

Mairead's Sticky Toffee Pudding with Hazelnut Toffee Sauce

This is my sister Mairead's recipe - she gave it to me as she thought that it would be a great seller at the market, and it was!

Serves 6

350g (12 oz) fresh dates, stoned (use dried dates if you can't find fresh)
300ml (10fl oz) boiling water
100g (3½ oz) butter
300g (10oz) dark brown sugar
3 medium eggs
400g (14 oz) self-raising flour, sieved
½ tsp bicarbonate of soda

For the hazelnut toffee sauce:

600ml (1 pint) double cream
250g (9oz) dark brown sugar
100g (3½ oz) butter
30g (1 oz) hazelnuts, roughly chopped

Place the dates in a saucepan with the boiling water, and simmer over a low heat for 15 minutes or until the dates are soft. Drain and then whizz the dates in a blender until they have a smooth consistency.

In a large mixing bowl, whisk the butter and sugar until creamy, then beat in the eggs, one at a time. Stir in the blended dates, then fold in the flour and bicarbonate of soda and mix well.

Grease a 20cm (8in) spring form tin and line it with greaseproof paper. Pour in the mixture and bake in a preheated oven at 170°C, 325°F, Gas Mark 3 for 1 hour.

Meanwhile, make the sauce. Pour half of the cream into a saucepan and stir in the brown sugar and butter. Bring to the boil, stirring frequently. When the sauce looks golden, stir in the remaining cream and half of the hazelnuts.

Turn out the cooked sponge onto a serving dish. Pour over the hazelnut toffee sauce and sprinkle the remaining hazelnuts on top. Delicious served with cream or vanilla ice cream.

Lemony Carrageen Moss Pots

For centuries seaweed has been part of the Irish diet, which is not really surprising given our coastline is over 3,000km (1,864 miles). It even sustained whole communities throughout the potato famine. Carrageen was used in soups, stews and puddings as a thickener. You can buy it in dried health food stores and it keeps for ages. This recipe is so light and delicious that it's perfect after a heavy dinner.

Makes 6 125ml (4½ fl oz) pots

8g (¼oz) carrageen moss
700ml (1¼ pints) milk
4 tbsp caster sugar
6 lemon balm leaves (or the
    grated zest of 3 lemons)
1 vanilla pod
2 eggs, separated
extra carrageen, to decorate

Soak the carrageen moss in lukewarm water for 15 minutes. Drain and place in a saucepan with the milk, 1 tablespoon of sugar, lemon balm and vanilla pod. Bring to the boil, then reduce the heat and simmer for 30 minutes. Strain through a sieve into a bowl, pushing the natural gelatine from the carrageen moss through the sieve.

Put the egg yolks in a bowl and beat in 3 tablespoons of sugar. Whisk in the strained milk mixture.

Whisk the egg whites until they form stiff peaks. Fold them into the mixture with a metal spoon. Use a figure of eight movement to get rid of any blobs of egg white. Fill 6 little pots with the mixture and chill in the fridge for about 1 hour or until set. Serve decorated with tiny sprigs of carrageen moss.

Regina Sexton's Curd Tart with Rosewater and Prunes

Regina Sexton and I spend hours together pouring over food books and travelling abroad to find new exciting foods. She is not only a brilliant scholar but also a wonderful friend. (See page 65 for more on Regina.)

Serves 8

50g (2oz) currants
4-6 prunes, torn in half and stoned
few drops of rosewater
225g (8oz) curds or cottage cheese
110g (4oz) ground almonds or
    crushed macaroons
30g (1oz) flaked almonds
110g (4oz) icing sugar
3 egg yolks, beaten
freshly grated nutmeg, to taste

200g (7oz) butter, melted and
    cooled slightly
egg white, for brushing

For the pastry:
175g (6oz) plain white flour
2 tsp icing sugar
75g (2½oz) butter
1 egg yolk, beaten

First, make the pastry. Sieve the flour and icing sugar into a bowl. Cut the butter into dice and rub it in with your fingertips until it resembles rough breadcrumbs. Stir in the egg yolk, working to bind the mixture to a soft dough.

Shape into a round, wrap in greaseproof paper and chill in the fridge for several hours or, preferably, overnight.

Soak the currants and prunes in the rosewater and leave to macerate overnight. Next day, mix together the cheese, ground almonds or macaroons, flaked almonds, sugar, egg yolks and nutmeg. Stir in the soaked fruit, then pour in the melted butter and mix well.

Roll out the pastry and line a greased 23cm (9in) cake tin which is 5cm (2in) deep. Line with greaseproof paper and fill with baking beans (or any dried beans) and bake for 15 minutes in a preheated oven at 180°C, 350°F, Gas Mark 4. Remove the beans and paper, and brush the sides and base of the pastry with egg white. Bake for a further 5 minutes.

Pour the cheese filling into the pastry case and bake for 45-50 minutes. Allow to cool before serving.

Richard GL's Pecan and Maple Syrup Shortbread Fingers

Richard Graham Leigh is the most fantastic pâtissier (read his profile on page 188). For a real shortbread, it is important to use flour without any raising agents, so unbleached white flour is best, also use unrefined muscovado sugar rather than just 'soft brown'.

Makes 12 fingers
300g (10 oz) pecan halves
110g (4 oz) unsalted butter
300g (10 1/2 oz) light muscovado sugar
125ml (4 1/2 fl oz) maple syrup
2 tsp natural vanilla essence
60ml (2 fl oz) single cream

For the shortbread base:
225g (8 oz) unsalted butter, at room temperature
100g (3 1/2 oz) caster sugar
280g (10 oz) unbleached flour

Place the pecan halves on a baking tray and place in a preheated oven at 180°C, 350°F, Gas Mark 4 for 10 minutes. Cool, then chop coarsely and set aside. Do not turn the oven off.

Make the shortbread base: beat the butter until soft in a food processor at medium speed, then add the sugar in a steady stream, mixing well. At slow speed, add the flour, a little at a time, and mix until a dough forms. Don't over-mix, or the shortbread will be tough rather than crumbly.

Spread out the dough evenly in a 20 x 30 x 2.5cm (8 x 12 x 1in) baking tin which has been lined with greaseproof or baking paper. It's quickest to press it into the tin and smooth it out with your fingertips through a piece of cling film. Or, you can form it into a ball and roll it out with a rolling pin - this gives a more even base. Bake in the preheated oven at 180°C, 350°F, Gas Mark 4 for about 15-20 minutes until the crust is lightly browned. Leave to cool on a cooling rack. Again, leave the oven on.

Meanwhile, in a saucepan melt the butter with the muscovado sugar and maple syrup, stirring until well mixed. Increase the heat and bring to a full boil, stirring all the time. Remove from the heat and add the vanilla essence and cream, then the chopped pecans. Pour on to the cooled shortbread base, spreading evenly, and bake in the preheated oven for 20-25 minutes. Remove to a cooling rack to cool completely. Handle with care, as the topping will still be liquid - and extremely hot - when you remove the tin from the oven. Store in an airtight container.

Rice Pudding with Jam

This was an old favourite at home when I was growing up. Kids absolutely adore it, and it's so easy to make.

Serves 4

10g butter
70g (2½ oz) short-grain
    pudding rice
1 litre (1¾ pints) milk

45g (1½ oz) caster sugar
a little freshly grated nutmeg or
    cinnamon
home-made raspberry jam, to serve

Grease a baking dish with butter, pour in the rice, add the milk and caster sugar, and stir. Grate some nutmeg or cinnamon on top.

Cook in a preheated oven at 150°C, 300°F, Gas Mark 2 for 1½ hours, stirring a couple of times, until the rice is tender and creamy and has absorbed most of the liquid. Serve hot with home-made raspberry jam.

Summer Berry Frozen Yogurt

During the summer months, an incredible range of Irish berries is available at the farmers' markets as well as some great locally produced yogurts, such as Glenilen and Knockadee Dairy. You can freeze the berries and use them in the winter.

Serves 4-6

300g (10 oz) mixed frozen
    berries (e.g. redcurrants,
    blackberries, raspberries,
    strawberries)

450ml (16fl oz) good-quality
    natural yogurt (chilled)
2 tbsp runny honey
1 sprig fresh mint

Take the frozen fruit out of the freezer and blend in a food processor for 10 seconds. Add the yogurt and honey and blend until smooth.

Place in a bowl or sealed container in the freezer for 1 hour or until frozen. Scoop into serving dishes and decorate each with a mint leaf.

Victoria Sandwich

Any good farmers' market will have an old-fashioned Victoria sponge for sale. They are perfect for Sunday afternoon tea.

Serves 8

110g (4oz) butter
110g (4oz) caster sugar
2 eggs
110g (4oz) self-raising flour, sieved
pinch of salt
1 tbsp warm water
a pot of home-made raspberry or strawberry jam
600ml (1 pint) whipped cream
icing sugar, for dusting

Beat together the butter and sugar until light and creamy, then beat in the eggs, one at a time. Add the sifted flour and salt with the warm water and mix well with a wooden spoon.

Divide the cake mixture between two 18cm (7in) sandwich tins lined with greaseproof paper and bake in a preheated oven at 190°C, 375°F, Gas Mark 5 for 15–20 minutes until well-risen and cooked through. Turn the sponges out onto a cooling rack and leave to cool.

Sandwich the sponges together with raspberry or strawberry jam and whipped cream. Dust with icing sugar and serve cut into slices.

Mini Pavlovas with Sweet Geranium-Infused Rhubarb

These pavlovas are just so cute and the taste is so decadent!

Makes 4 small or 1 large
3 egg whites
175g (6 oz) caster sugar
1 tsp cornflour
1 tsp white wine vinegar
½ tsp vanilla extract
whipped cream

For the rhubarb:
150g (5 oz) rhubarb, cut into
    5cm (2 in) sections
50g (2 oz) caster sugar
2 sweet geranium leaves
    (see tip)
70ml (2½ fl oz) water

Line a baking sheet with non-stick baking paper. Whisk the egg whites in a large, clean bowl until stiff, and then whisk in the sugar gradually until the egg whites have a glossy shine. Fold in the cornflour, vinegar and vanilla extract.

Divide the meringue mixture into 4 heaps on the baking paper and, with a spoon, shape and swirl each one into a circle, leaving a dip in the centre. (Alternatively, you can make 1 large pavlova by spooning the meringue onto the baking paper in 1 heap.) Cook in a preheated oven at 150°C, 300°, Gas Mark 2 for 40 minutes until the meringue is pale brown and dry on the outside but soft on the inside.

Meanwhile, stew the rhubarb gently with the sugar, sweet geranium leaves and water in a covered pan, until the rhubarb is cooked but not mushy. Leave to cool.

Arrange the individual pavlovas on 4 serving plates. Place a big dollop of whipped cream in the centre of each one and then arrange the rhubarb on top. Serve with the sweet stewing liquid.

Tip: If you don't have any sweet geranium leaves you can use lemon balm leaves instead, but it's well worth hunting them out or growing your own. Use any spare leaves as a decorative garnish.

Chocolate

It will come as no surprise to dedicated chocolate addicts that the botanical name for chocolate, *Theobroma cacao*, comes from the Aztec word meaning 'food of the Gods'. The Aztecs originally drank it with chilli. No need to go to Mexico for your nectar when we have such fine chocolatiers at home selling through farmers' markets and delicatessens.

Chocolate is made from the fermented, roasted and ground beans taken from the pod of the tropical cacao tree, native to Central America. Cocoa is the solid part of the bean and cocoa butter is the fat component. Chocolate bars are made by combining the solids and fat from the bean with the addition of sugar and other ingredients, and it is the proportions of this combination that influences the taste. There is a world of difference between fine chocolate and all the rest, here are the main categories:

- Dark chocolate: chocolate without milk as an additive; sometimes called plain chocolate. European rules specify a minimum of 35% cocoa solids.
- Milk chocolate: chocolate with milk powder or condensed milk added. European rules specify a minimum of 25% cocoa solids.
- White chocolate: chocolate based on cocoa butter without the cocoa solids.
- Semi-sweet chocolate: used for cooking purposes; a dark chocolate with higher sugar content and often lower cocoa content than true dark chocolate.
- Couverture: this is the finest quality chocolate rich in cocoa butter and at least 70% chocolate liquor content, with pure vanilla added, not vanilla flavouring. But the real distinction is the variety of cocoa bean: couverture is made from the superior Criollo bean (the bulk cocoa bean is the inferior Forastero bean). This is the chocolate that is often compared to fine wine because of the subtlety of taste!
- Artisan chocolate is distinctive from run of the mill chocolate for a number of reasons. Firstly, it is in the way they process the cocoa beans. Conching is where the kernels, extracted from the beans, are kneaded to release moisture and improve texture and flavour. Commercial chocolate is conched for 12–24 hours. Secondly, artisan chocolate-makers will use couverture – the finest quality chocolate. Finally Artisan chocolate-makers have the imagination and the freedom to experiment, which makes their product unique.

Among our many artisan chocolatiers are sisters Sarah Hehir and Emily Sandford who started The Cocoa Bean Artisan Chocolate Company in 2002 from their kitchen in Limerick. They began selling their chocolates from a stall in Limerick Market and quickly made a name for themselves as specialists in dark chocolate. Now they have a workshop in Limerick but stay true to their artisan production methods: sourcing the finest and freshest ingredients, seeking out new and exciting taste combinations, and sourcing locally whenever possible. Incidentally, they conch their chocolate for up to seven days, giving it a wonderful velvety finish and a rounded, balanced flavour.

Sarah and Emily give traditional chocolates a lift by adding the finest possible ingredients. Their divine vanilla chocolate is infused with generous amounts of Madagascan vanilla pods, and their orange chocolate contains freshly grated zest. They maintain a constant quest for new and stimulating flavours. This has led them to award-winning combinations such as lime zest and black pepper, and tamarind with star anise and ginger. Even their packaging is sourced from small family businesses. The wrappers are vibrant funky colours and each chocolate is individually hand wrapped: a fitting end for a damn fine chocolate!

There are many fantastic chocolate-makers that you will see at the farmers' market. The O'Connaill family from Cork have a superb selection of hand-made chocolates, as do Eve's and Aines.

Hot Chocolate Puddings with Blackberries

I make these little puddings in china cups or bowls because they look so pretty. The hot chocolate usually pours out of the top like a volcano - it's very impressive!

Makes 6

200g (7 oz) dark chocolate
    (70% cocoa solids)
200g (7 oz) butter
4 eggs, plus 4 egg yolks
    (reserve the whites for
    pavlova, see page 200)
110g (4 oz) caster sugar
60g (2 oz) plain flour
300g (10oz) blackberries
extra caster sugar, to serve

Melt the chocolate and butter together over a low heat. While they are melting, beat the eggs, egg yolks and sugar together in a bowl. Beat in the melted chocolate, then fold in the flour and the blackberries (holding back 6 for decoration).

Pour the chocolate mixture into 6 greased individual moulds and cook in a preheated oven at 180°C, 350°F, Gas Mark 4 for 10 minutes.

Just before you serve top each pudding with a reserved blackberry.

Chocolate Truffles

Make these little lovelies for dessert and serve with a scoop of vanilla ice cream.

Makes 30

200g (7 oz) dark chocolate (at least 70% cocoa solids), broken into pieces

200ml (7 fl oz) double cream

cocoa powder, for dusting

Slowly melt the chocolate until it is smooth and glossy in a bowl suspended over a pan of simmering water. Meanwhile, gently heat the cream in a saucepan until warm. Pour the warm cream onto the melted chocolate and mix well until incorporated. Set aside to cool and firm up.

Once firm, take teaspoons of the mixture, dust with cocoa powder and roll into balls. Leave to set in the fridge.

Easy Florentines

These are the simplest thing in the world to make. They melt very quickly so just make sure that you keep them in the fridge until you are about to serve.

Makes 24

100g (3½ oz) dark chocolate

100g (3½ oz) milk chocolate

100g (3½ oz) white chocolate

110g (4 oz) flaked almonds

150g (5 oz) raisins

125g (4½ oz) glacé cherries

Melt the chocolates very slowly in separate bowls, each suspended over a pan of simmering water.

Take teaspoons of the melted chocolates and spread each one onto sheets of greaseproof or baking paper, to form even-sized discs. Sprinkle the chocolate discs with flaked almonds, raisins and cherries and place in the fridge for about 2 hours to allow the Florentines to set.

Chocolate Biscuit Cake

Any market you visit in Ireland will have this for sale. It's really easy to make, keeps well and, most importantly, tastes great with a cuppa.

Makes 9-12, depending
on how big you cut your squares
175g (6oz) butter
2 tbsp golden syrup
250g (9oz) dark chocolate (55-70%
cocoa solids), cut into pieces
280g (10oz) rich tea biscuits
85g (3oz) raisins
85g (3oz) chopped roasted hazelnuts

Lightly grease a 23cm (9in) cake tin.

Melt the butter, golden syrup and chocolate in a bowl in the microwave or in a heavy-bottomed saucepan over a very low heat, then stir until smooth.

Crush the biscuits with a rolling pin, but leave some slightly larger chunks, and tip into the melted chocolate mixture with the raisins and hazelnuts. Stir well.

Spoon the chocolate mixture into the prepared tin, pressing it down well to get a smooth, even surface. When cool, chill in the fridge, then serve cut into squares.

Chocolate Bread and Butter Pudding

Bread and chocolate are two of my favourite things. This moist, rich, comforting dessert is a decadent take on an old favourite.

Serves 6
400ml (14fl oz) single cream
400ml (14fl oz) milk
100g (3½oz) caster sugar
150g (5oz) dark chocolate
    (70% cocoa solids), broken
    into squares
6 eggs
14 x 1cm (½in) slices of brioche

In a saucepan, mix together the cream, milk and sugar. Gently heat through, stirring occasionally, until the sugar dissolves. Set aside to cool.

Melt the chocolate in a heatproof bowl suspended over a pan of simmering water. Mix the melted chocolate into the cooled milk mixture.

Break the eggs into a large mixing bowl, pour in the chocolate mixture and lightly whisk together. Place the sliced brioche, slightly overlapping the slices, in a large shallow ovenproof dish. Pour over the chocolate mixture.

Bake in a preheated oven at 150°C, 300°F, Gas Mark 2 for 45 minutes.

Murphy's White Chocolate and Rosewater Ice Cream

Sean and Kieran Murphy very kindly gave me this delicious recipe. Their ice cream contains fresh Kerry cream, fresh milk, high-quality Belgian chocolate, their own home-made caramel, pure Bourbon, real rum and Irish whiskey - the list goes on. If you are lucky enough to be in Dingle, you can buy it at their shop on Sraid na Tra. This recipe is a decadently rich, French custard-style ice cream for white chocolate lovers, with a sweet floral hint. Use good-quality chocolate if you want a good result!

Serves 6

100g (3½ oz) white chocolate	260ml (9 fl oz) milk
225g (8 oz) caster sugar	¼ tsp rosewater
5 egg yolks	¼ tsp pure vanilla extract
	260ml (9 fl oz) double cream

Melt the chocolate in a bowl suspended over a saucepan of simmering water.

Beat the sugar and egg yolks together until they are creamy and a pale yellow.

Heat the milk to a bare simmer, then remove from the heat and beat into the egg and sugar mixture, pouring in a slow stream. Pour the mixture back into the pan and place over a low heat. Stir until the custard thickens.

Add the custard to the melted chocolate, a little at a time, mixing thoroughly until smooth and velvety. Leave to cool, then mix in the rosewater and vanilla. Whip the cream and gently fold into the chocolate custard.

Freeze and churn using a domestic ice cream machine, or cover and place in the freezer until frozen. (If using the manual method, take the mixture out and stir with a fork occasionally.)

Tips:
- Rosewater is not the same as rose essence – rose essence is much stronger!
- The chocolate and the custard should both be warm when you mix them for a good emulsion. The chocolate will clump at first when you add the liquid, but keep on adding and stirring, and it will come smooth.

Directory

Great places to Eat and Stay in Ireland

Cork City

Café Paradiso
Restaurant and Rooms
16 Lancaster Quay, Cork
Tel: 00 353 (0) 21 4277939
www.cafeparadiso.ie
The food is so fantastic here it would never even cross your mind that it's vegetarian. Upstairs they have recently added on 3 incredibly stylish rooms for overnighters, so you never have to leave!

Boqueria, Tapas Bar
Bridge St., Cork
Prop. Jerry
Tel: 00 353 (0) 21 4559049
Great place to go for a delicious glass of wine and beautiful tapas using local produce from Cork.

Farmgate
The English Market, Cork
Tel: 00 353 (0) 21 4278134
Traditional Irish dishes.
This is proper comfort food at its best! Shepherd's pie, stews, crumbles, bread and butter puddings all made on the premises.

Fast Al's Pizzas
Paradise Place, Cork City
This is a great place to grab a really good slice of pizza, it's a tiny shop on a corner but if you are wandering around the city and you want to fill a gap this is your spot!

West Cork

Fishy Fishy
Kinsale, West Cork
Tel: 00 353 (0) 21 477 4453
Delicious fresh fish cooked simply but beautifully.

Deasy's Pub
Ring, West Cork
Tel: 00 353 (0) 23 35741
Fresh fish, local cheese and meats, seasonal vegetables, and a view over the water – could you ask for more?

Hackett's Pub
Main St., Schull, West Cork
Tel: 00 353 (0) 28 28625
Great pub food using all the famous cheeses, smoked fish and charcuterie from West Cork.

The Good Things Café
Durrus
West Cork
Tel: 00 353 (0) 27 61426
Delicious pizzas topped with local cheeses; fresh fish delivered daily; warming soups.

East Cork

Ballymaloe House
Cloyne, East Cork
Tel: 00 353 (0) 21 4652 531
Incredible local and seasonal food cooked to perfection and served in the most decadent of surroundings.

The Farmgate
Midleton, East Cork
Tel: 00 353 (0) 21 463 2771
During the day, the food here is comfort food at its best. In the evening it is a bit more sophisticated but still simple and delicious. They also have a shop at the front of the restaurant where you can buy great olive oils, local honeys, farmhouse cheeses and their daily baked bread and cakes.

Waterford

The Tannery
Quay St., Dungarven, Co. Waterford
Tel: 00 353 (0) 58 45420
Contemporary Irish cuisine using the best of what Irish producers have to offer. They now have a beautiful townhouse across the road where you can rest your weary self after a fabulous feast.

Dublin

Chapter One
Parnell Square, Dublin 1
Tel: 00 353 (0) 1 873 2266
An oasis of fantastic food in the middle of the city. Stylish, delicious, innovative are words that spring to mind. They do a great pre-theatre menu.

Gruel
Dame St., Dublin 2
Tel: 00 353 (0) 1 670 7119
Casual, hip and fantastic food with a menu that changes daily. But when you are leaving don't forget to grab one of their chocolate brownies from the take-away counter, you'll regret it if you don't!

Avoca
Suffolk St., Dublin 1
Tel: 00 353 (0) 1 672 6019
Kilmacanogue, Co. Wicklow
Tel: 00 353 (0) 1 286 7466
Delicious seasonal salads, pizzas, pies and home baking

Mackerel
Bewleys Café,
78–79 Grafton St,
Dublin 2
Tel: 00 353 (0) 1 6727719
A fantastic range of fish cooked creatively.

Tipperary

Country Choice
Main St., Nenagh
Tel: 00 353 (0) 67 32596
It's a great place to stop for lunch or a afternoon snack, you will feast on home-cooked meats, beautiful salads, farmhouse cheeses and pâtés. You can also buy everything that you just ate in their wonderful shop out front.

Galway

Sheridans on the Docks
Galway City
Fabulous gastro pub serving delicious sandwiches, stews and farmhouse cheese and charcuterie plates.

List of Farmers' Markets in Ireland

Antrim

Origin Farmers' Market Ballymoney
Castlecroft, Main St
Last Saturday of month 11-2pm
Joanne McLaughlin, Ballymoney Town
Centre Mgt - 00 44 (0) 28 27660238
(048 from ROI)

City Food And Garden Market Belfast
St George's Street
Saturday 9-4pm
Jilly Dougan, Moyallon Foods
00 44 (0) 771 429 5947

Templepatrick
Colmans Garden Centre
Sean McArdle - 00 44 (0) 87 6115016
info@irishfarmersmarkets.ie

Lisburn Market
Saturday

Armagh

Portadown Market
Last Saturday of month

Carlow

Carlow
Potato Market Carlow
Saturday 9-2pm
John Hayden - 00 353 (0) 59 9133457
cando@eircom.net

Clare

Ballyvaughan
The Old Schoolhouse
Jenny Morton - 00 353 (0) 65 7077941

Ennis
Car Park, Upr Main Street
Friday 8-2pm
Alan Johnston - 00 353 (0) 91 631035
ennisfarmers@eircom.net

Killaloe
Between the Waters
Sunday 11-3pm
Bronagh Moriarty
00 353 (0) 86 8857290

Kilrush
The Square
Thursday 9-2pm
Michael Gleeson - 00 353 (0) 87 2272115
michael.gleeson@eiri.org

Shannon
Drumgeely Shopping Area
Friday 12.30-7pm
Padraig MacCromaic, Shannon Town
Council - pmccormaic@clarecoco.ie

Cork

Ballincollig
Village shopping centre
Wednesday 10am-2pm

Ballydehob Food Market
Community Hall
Friday 10.30-12pm

Bandon Market
Bandon
Friday 10.30-1pm

Bantry Market
Main Square
1st Friday of month

Blackwater Valley
Nano Nagle Centre, Mallow
Every 2nd Saturday 10.30-1pm
Mary Sleeman - 00 353 (0) 22 25250
marysleeman@eircom.net

Castletownbere
1st Thursday of month

Clonakilty
McCurtain Hill
Thursdays & Sundays 10-2pm
Ellie Morgan - 00 353 (0) 23 48749

Cobh Market
Seafront
Friday 10-1pm

Cornmarket Street Market
Cornmarket Street
Saturday 9-3pm
Caroline Robinson - 00 353 (0) 21 7330178
carolinerobinson@eircom.net

Douglas Food Market
Douglas Community Park
Saturday 9.30-2pm
Rose Farrell - 00 353 (0) 86 3693759

Dunmanway
The Old Mill, Castle St
Fridays 10-2pm

English Market
Entrances on Princes St & Grand Parade
Daily
Sean Healy - 00 353 (0) 86 2400153 /
www.cork-guide.ie/cork_city/english-market

Fermoy
Opposite Cork Marts
Saturday 9-1pm
David Booth - 00 353 (0) 25 27577

Inchigeelagh Market
Creedons Hotel
Last Saturday of month
Fred La Haye - 00 353 (0) 26 47985

Kanturk
Indoors at the rear of Supervalue
Thursdays and Saturdays from 10.30am
Maura Kavanagh 00 353 (0) 87 9627776

Kinsale
Market Place
Tuesday, 9.30-2pm

Mahon Point
West Entrance
Mahon Point Shopping Centre
Thursday 10-2pm
Rupert Hugh Jones - 00 353 (0) 86 1685312
rupert@ballycottonorganics.com

Macroom
The Square
Tuesday 9-3pm
UCD Office, Macroom

Midleton
Hospital Road
Saturday
Darina Allen - 00 353 (0) 251 4646785
www.midletonfarmersmarket.com

Mitchelstown
Main Square
Saturday 9-1pm
David Minton - 00 353 (0) 25 85213 / 00
353 (0) 86 1050997

Schull
Car park near pier
Sunday 10-3pm
Fingal Ferguson - 00 353 (0) 28 27824

Skibbereen
Old Market Square
Saturday 10-2pm
Madeline McKeever
madsmckeever@eircom.net
www.westcorkweb.ie/market/index

Derry
Guildhall Country Fair
Last Saturday in month
David Hawthorne - 00 44 (0) 7776 471056

Donegal
Ballybofey
GAA grounds
Friday 12-4pm
Frank Kelly - 00 353 (0) 86 8178854

Down
Newry Dundalk
Newry Marketplace, John Mitchell Place
Friday 9am 2pm
Florence van Dijk
00 44 (0) 28 3026 9095
(048 from ROI)

Dublin
Dalkey Market
Dalkey Town Hall
Friday 10-4pm
Jackie Spillane - 00 353 (0) 87 9573647
market@dlrcoco.ie

Dundrum
Airfield House
Saturday 10-4pm
Sean McArdle - 00 353 (0) 87 6115016
info@irishfarmersmarkets.ie

Dunlaoghaire Harbour Market
DunLaoghaire Harbour
Saturday 10-4pm
Sean McArdle - 00 353 (0) 87 6115016
info@irishfarmersmarkets.ie

DunLaoghaire People's Park Market
People's Park
Sunday 11-4pm
Jackie Spillane - 00 353 (0) 87 9573647
market@dlrcoco.ie

DunLaoghaire Shopping Centre
DunLaoghaire Shopping Centre
Thursdays 10-5pm
Jackie Spillane - 00 353 (0) 87 9573647
market@dlrcoco.ie

Farmleigh Food Market
Farmleigh House
2006 dates TBC
Dave Levins, OPW - dave.levins@opw.ie

Fingal Food Fayre
Fingal Arts Centre
Last Sunday every month 12-5pm
Vera Tyrell - 00 353 (0) 1 8437567
fingalartcentre@eircom.net

Howth Harbour Market
The Harbour, Howth
Sunday 10-3pm
Sean McArdle - 00 353 (0) 87 6115016
info@irishfarmersmarkets.ie

Leopardstown
Leopardstown Racecourse
Friday 11-7pm
Sean McArdle - 00 353 (0) 87 6115016
info@irishfarmersmarkets.ie

Malahide Market
GAA facility, Church Rd
Saturday 11-5pm
Sean McArdle - 00 353 (0) 87 6115016
info@irishfarmersmarkets.ie

Marley Park Food Market
Marlay Park Craft Courtyard
Saturday 10-4pm
Jackie Spillane - 00 353 (0) 87 9573647
market@dlrcoco.ie

Monkstown Village Market
Monkstown Parish Church
Saturday 10-4pm
Tara Dalton - 00 353 (0) 87 2349419
info@monkstownvillagemarket.com

Pearse Street Market
St Andrews Centre
Saturday 9.30-3pm
Padraig Cannon - 00 353 (0) 1 8730451
dfc@clubi.ie

Ranelagh Market
Multi Denominational School
Sunday 10-4pm
Sean McArdle - 00 353 (0) 87 6115016
info@irishfarmersmarkets.ie

Temple Bar Market
Meeting House Square
Saturday 9-5pm
Temple Bar Properties - 00 353 (0)
1 6672255
info@temple-bar.ie

Ballinasloe
Croffy's Centre, Main Street
Fridays, 10-3pm
Úna Ní Bhroin, Beechlawn Organic Farm -
info@beechlawnfarm.org

Galway
Galway Market
Beside St Nicholas Church
Saturday, 8.30-4pm & Sunday 2-6pm
galwaymarket@eircom.net

Kerry
Cahirciveen Market
Community Centre
Thursday 10-2pm (Jun-Sept)
Barbara Cassidy - 00 353 (0) 87 2965874

Caherdaniel Market
Village Hall
Friday 10-12am (Jun-Sept & Christmas)
Jane Maher - 00 353 (0) 66 9475479

Dingle Farm Produce & Craft Market
by the fishing harbour near bus stop
Friday 9.30-4pm
Jill Sanderson - 00 353 (0) 66 9157346

Kenmare
Wed - Sun 10-6pm (7 days Jul-Aug)
Vince - 00 353 (0) 86 3128262

Listowel Food Fair
Seanchai Centre
Thursday 10-1pm
Joanna Watkins - 00 353 (0) 68 23034
listowelfoodfair@eircom.net
www.listowelfoodfair.com

Milltown Market
Old Church
Sat 10-2pm
Mary O'Riordan - 00 353 (0) 66 9767869
www.milltownorganicmarket.com

Milltown Market
Organic Centre
Tuesday - Friday, 2-5pm
Mary O'Riordan - 00 353 (0) 66 9767869
www.milltownorganicmarket.com

Sneem Market
Community Centre
Tuesday 11-2pm (Jun-Sept & Christmas)
Jill House - oo 353 (o) 66 9475312

Tralee
Friday 9-5pm

Athy
Emily Square
Sunday 10-2pm
www.kildare.ie/athyfarmersmarket

Larchill Market
Larchill Arcadian Gardens
3rd Sunday in month
Sean McArdle - oo 353 (o) 87 6115016
info@irishfarmersmarkets.ie

Naas
The Storehouse Restaurant
Saturday 10-3pm
Siobhan Poppelwell - oo 353 (o) 87 6080119
siobhanpoppelwell@ireland.com

Newbridge
The Courtyard Shopping Centre
Friday 10-3pm
Siobhan Poppelwell - oo 353 (o) 87 6080119
siobhanpoppelwell@ireland.com

Kilkenny
Kilkenny
Gowran Park
1st & 3rd Sunday of month
Sean McArdle - oo 353 (o) 87 6115016
info@irishfarmersmarkets.ie

Leitrim
**Origin
(Manorhamilton)**
Beepark Resource Centre
Last Friday of each month
Gerard Creamer - oo 353 (o) 71 9856935

Limerick
Abbeyfeale
Parish Hall
Friday 9-1pm
Marion Harnett - oo 353 (o) 87 6866450

Kilmallock
The Kilmallock GAA Club
Friday 9-1pm
Joe Biggane - oo 353 (o) 63 91300

Limerick Milk Market
Limerick Milk Market
Saturday 8-1.30pm
Brendan Woods - oo 353 (o) 86 8098400

Longford
Longford
Temperance Hall
Saturday 9.30-1pm
Marian Carthy - oo 353 (o) 43 24862 /
oo 353 (o) 86 8560576

Louth
Castlebellingham
Bellingham Castle Hotel
1st Sunday of month
Janette Behan - oo 353 (o) 86 6060277

Newry Dundalk
The County Museum, Jocelyn Street,
Dundalk
Saturday 10am-2pm
Florence van Dijk - oo 44 (o) 28 3026 9095
(048 from ROI)

Meath
Kells
FBD Insurance Grounds
Saturday 10-2pm
Barry Brennan - oo 353 (o) 46 8246025

Monaghan
Monaghan Farmers / Country Market
Castleblayney Livestock Salesyard
Last Saturday of month , 9-1pm
Maura Nugent - oo 353 (o) 42 9740712

Offaly
The Full Moon Market
The Chestnut Courtyard
Every 3rd Sunday
Andreena Purcell

Offaly
Tullamore Country Fair
Millenium Square
Saturday 9-4pm
Tommy Corrigan - oo 353 (o) 87 2792615

Roscommon
Origin (Boyle)
Grounds of King House
Saturday, 10-2pm
Patricia Golden - oo 353 (o) 71 9663033
unabhan@indigo.ie

Sligo
Origin (Sligo)
Sligo IT Sports Field Car Park
Saturday
Michael McPadden - oo 353 (o) 87 2351066

Tipperary
Cahir
Beside The Craft Granary
Saturday 9-1pm
Pat O'Brien - oo 353 (o) 86 6482044 /
pbobrien7@eircom.net

Clonmel
St Peter&Paul's Primary School, Kickham
Street, beside Oakville Shopping Centre
Saturday 10-2pm
Bernie Lennon - oo 353 (o) 86 2937220

Tipperary
Carrick-on-Suir
Heritage Centre, Main St
Friday 10-2pm
Stella Coffey - oo 353 (o) 52 42816

Nenagh
Teach an Lean
1st Saturday of month 10-2pm
Cllr Sandra Farrell - oo 353 (o) 87 6988401

Tyrone
Origin, Strabane
The Score Centre, Dock Rd
Last Saturday of month
Strabane Farmers Forum - oo 44 (o) 28
71880680
(048 from ROI)

Tyrone
Tesco Carpark, Dungannon
1st Saturday of month 8.30-1pm
Irene Molloy - oo 44 (o) 48 37523752
irene@initiative.ie
www.tyronefarmersmarket.com

Waterford

Dunhill
Parish Hall
Last Sunday of month 11.30-2pm
Catherine Kelleher

Dungarvan
Scanlon's Yard (beside Friary St & Mary St)
Thursday 9.30-2pm
Siobhan La Touche - 00 353 (0) 86 3940564

Lismore
Blackwater Valley

Stradbally Community Market
1st Saturday of month 10-12.30pm

Waterford
Jenkins Lane
Saturday 10-4pm
Sinead Cheevers - 00 353 (0) 87 9398813
bbbread@gofree.indigo.ie

Westmeath

Athlone Farmers Market
Market Square, Athlone
Saturday 10-3pm
Andrew McGuinness - 00 353 (0)
86-8844938
andrew.mcguinness@hotmail.com

Westmeath

Mullingar Farmers Market
Harbour Place Shopping Centre
1st & 3rd Sunday of Month
Sheena Shanley - 00 353 (0) 87 66447909
sheenashanley@eircom.net

Wexford

New Ross
Conduit Lane
Saturday 9-2pm
Denis Shannon - 00 353 (0) 87 4114481
alltheshannons@eircom.net

Wexford Farmers Market Dunbrody
Dunbrody Abbey Centre
Sunday 12-3.30pm
Pierce McAuliffe - 00 353 (0) 51 388933
www.cookingireland.com

Wexford Farmers Market Community
Partnership
The Abbey Square Carpark
Saturday 9-2pm
Denis Shannon - 00 353 (0) 87 4114481
alltheshannons@eircom.net

Wexford Farmers Market
Trimmers Lane West (beside La Dolce Vita
Restaurant)
Friday 9-2pm
Denis Shannon - 00 353 (0) 87 4114481
alltheshannons@eircom.net

Wicklow

Brooklodge Organic Market
Macreddin Village
1st & 3rd Sunday of month
Evan Doyle - 00 353 (0) 402 36444
brooklodge@macreddin.ie

Glendalough
Brockagh Resource Centre
2nd Sunday of month 11-6pm
Sean McArdle - 00 353 (0) 87 6115016
info@irishfarmersmarkets.ie

Kilcoole
Saturdays - 10.30 - 11.30am

Powerscourt Waterfall Market
Farmyard, almost next to Powerscourt
Waterfall
2nd and 4th Sunday of every month
Liz - 00 353 (0) 86 8244786
ekeegan2004@eircom. net

Bray
Killarney Road near the Boghall Road
Saturday 10-3pm
Jackie Spillane - 00 353 (0) 87 9573647
market@dlrcoco.ie

Bray Seafront Market
Albert Avenue, just across from the
aquarium
Friday & Sunday weekly
David Molony - info@market.ie
00 353 (0) 86 683 9156

List of Producers

Bakery

Arbutus Breads, Cork City
Artisan breads
Tel: 00 353 (0) 21 4501113
E-mail: arbutus@iol.ie

Alternative Bread Company, Cork City
Handmade breads
Tel: 00 353 (0) 21 489 7787

Soul Bakery, Co. Dublin
Handmade breads
Tel: 00 353 (0) 86 8184705
www.soulbakery.ie

La Maison Des Gourmets, Dublin
French-style breads
Tel: 00 353 (0) 1 672 7258

Richard Graham Leigh Patisserie,
Drimoleague, West Cork
French style tarts, biscuits, and cakes
Tel: 00 353 (0) 86 086 8183
E-mail: rglpatisserie@eircom.net

The Yew Tree, Co. Galway
Freshly baked breads
Tel: 00 353 (0) 91 866886

George Heise's Patisserie, Co. Meath
Fine patisserie
Tel: 00 353 (0) 41 982 4493

Baking Emporium, Dunmanway, West Cork
Crackers and crisp breads
Tel: 00 353 (0) 23 45260

Heavens Cake, The Old English Market, Cork
French-style tarts and cakes
Tel: 00 353 (0) 21 4222775

Unglert's Bakery, Ennistymon, Co. Clare
Breads and cakes
Tel: 00 353 (0) 65 707 1217

Gallic Kitchen, Dublin
Savoury and sweet pastries
Tel: 00 353 (0) 1 454 4912

The Great American Cookie Company
American-style cookies
Tel: 00 353 (0) 424 462

Leslie's Bakery, Co. Fermanagh
Regional handmade breads
Tel: 00 44 (0) 28 6632 4902

Ditty's Bakery, Co. Londonderry
Artisan breads, cakes and biscuits
Tel: 00 44 (0) 28 7946 8243
E-mail: dittybky@aol.com

Hunter's Bakery, Co. Londonderry
Artisan breads
Tel: 00 44 (0) 28 7772 2411

Dairy

Ardsallagh Goats Cheese, East Cork
Soft, hard and smoked goat's cheese
Tel: 00 353 (0) 21 488 2336

Sheridans
11 South Anne St.
Dublin 2
Tel: 00 353 (0) 1 679 3143
Fax: 00 353 (0) 1 679 3132

7 Pembroke Lane
Ballsbridge
Dublin 4
Tel: 00 353 (0) 1 660 8231
Fax: 00 353 (0) 1 660 8231

14-16 Churchyard St.
Galway
Tel: 00 353 (0) 91 564 829
Fax: 00 353 (0) 91 567 507

Wine Shop Upstairs
14-16 Churchyard St.
Galway
Tel: 00 353 (0) 91 564 829
Fax: 00 353 (0) 91 567 507

Bluebell Falls Goat's Cheese, Co. Clare
Soft goat's cheese
Tel: 00 353 (0) 65 683 8024

Coolea Farmhouse Cheese, Co. Cork
Gouda-style aged cow's milk cheese
Tel: 00 353 (0) 26 45204

St. Ola Goat's Cheese, Co. Clare
Soft and hard goat's cheese
Tel: 00 353 (0) 65 683 6633

Durrus Farmhouse Cheese, Durrus, West Cork
Raw-milk, semi-soft cheese
Tel: 00 353 (0) 27 61100/61017
www.durruscheese.com

Cooleeney Cheese, Co. Tipperary
Raw-milk cow's cheese, soft
Tel: 00 353 (0) 504 45112
cooleeney@eircom.net

Wicklow Farmhouse Cheese, Co. Wicklow
Blue-veined soft cheese
Tel: 00 353 (0) 402 39543

Knocklara, Co. Waterford
Sheep's cheese, soft and crumbly
Tel: 00 353 (0) 24 96326

Gubbeen Cheese, Schull, West Cork
Semi-soft - smoked and unsmoked
Tel: 00 353 (0) 28 28231
www.gubbeen.com

Croghan Farmhouse Cheese, Co. Wexford
Raw goat's milk cheese, soft and hard
Tel: 00 353 (0) 52 27 331

Carrigbyrne Farmhouse Cheese, Co. Wexford
Cow's milk, brie
Tel: 00 353 (0) 54 40560
E-mail: prb@iol.ie

Dingle Peninsula Cheese
Raw-milk cow's cheese with seaweed
Tel: 00 353 (0) 66 713 9028
www.dinglepeninsulacheese.com
Available at following markets: Dingle on Friday, Kenmare on Wednesday, Limerick on Saturday, Fota House in Cork once a month and the English Market in Cork. Also sold at Corleggy Cheese Stall, Temple Bar Market, Dublin

Hegarty's Cheddar, Whitechurch, Cork
Cheddar cheese
Tel: 00 353 (0) 21 488 4238

Gabriel and Desmond Cheese, Schull, West Cork
Hard, raw-milk cheese
Tel: 00 353 (0) 28 28593/28593
www.wcnc.ie

Corleggy Farmhouse Cheese
Raw-milk cow's cheese, goat's cheese and
raw sheep's cheese
Tel: 00 353 (0) 49 952 2930
www.corleggy.com

Ardrahan, Kanturk, Co. Cork
Semi-soft cow's cheese
Tel: 00 353 (0) 29 78099/29 78136
E-mail: ardrahancheese@eircom.net

Bluebell Falls Goats Cheese
Soft goat's cheese
Tel: 00 353 (0) 65 683 8024

Cashel Blue, Fethard, Co. Tipperary
Soft blue cheese
Tel: 00 353 (0) 52 31151/52 31066
E-mail: jlgrubb@eircom.net

Bellingham Blue Cheese, Co. Louth
Soft blue cheese
Tel: 00 353 (0) 42 937 2343

Milleens Cheese, Beara, Co. Cork
Tel: 00 353 (0) 27 74079/27 74379
E-mail: milleens@eircom.net

Cratloe Hills Sheep Cheese
Mature soft sheep's cheese
Tel: 00 353 (0) 61 357 185

Lavistown Farmhouse Cheese
Tel: 00 353 (0) 56 776 5145
www.lavistownhouse.ie

Oisin Farmhouse Cheese
Soft and hard goat's cheese and feta
Tel: 00 353 (0) 63 91528

Glenilen Farm, Drimoleague, Co. Cork
Butter, yogurts, clotted cream, fromage
frais, cheesecakes, mousses
Tel: 00 353 (0) 28 31179
E-mail: glenilenfarm@eircom.net

Knockatee Dairy, Co. Kerry
Butter, cheeses and yogurts
Tel: 00 353 (0) 64 84236

Murphy's Ice Cream, Co. Kerry
Handmade ice-creams
Tel: 00 353 (0) 66 915 2644
www.murphysicecream.com

**Tipperary Organic Ice-cream, Co.
Tipperary**
Handmade organic ice-cream
Tel: 00 353 (0) 52 81905

Growers

**Caroline Robinson, Templemartin,
Co. Cork**
Chemical-free vegetables
Tel: 00 353 (0) 21 733 0178

Denis Healy, Co. Wicklow
Organic vegetables and fruit (importer
and grower)
Tel: 00 353 (0) 59 6473193

Cait Curran, Co. Galway
Organic vegetables
Tel: 00 353 (0) 91 844 973
E-mail: ccurran@ireland.com

Ballintubber Farm, East Cork
Home-grown vegetables
Tel: 00 353 (0) 21 488 3034

Dirks Vegetables, Co. Galway
Organic vegetables
Tel: 00 353 (0) 65 707 8140

Glenties Farm, Co. Donegal
Bio-dynamic and organic vegetables
Tel: 00 353 (0) 74 955 1286

Derryvilla Farm, Co. Offaly
Fresh blueberries, tonics and relishes
Tel: 00 353 (0) 502 43945
www.derryvillablueberries.com

The Irish Seed Savers Association
www.irishseedsavers.ie

The Apple Farm, Co. Tipperary
Season fruit
Tel: 00 353 (0) 52 41459
www.theapplefarm.com

**Glenribben Organic Farm, Co.
Waterford**
Organic fruit and vegetables
Tel: 00 353 (0) 58 54860

Gold River Farm, Co. Wicklow
Organic fruit and vegetables
Tel: 00 353 (0) 402 36 426

**Marc Michel Organic Farm and Cafe,
Co. Wicklow**
Organic vegetables
Tel: 00 353 (0) 1 201 1882

Penny and Udo Lange, Co.Wicklow
Biodynamic-grown vegetables and fruit
Tel: 00 353 (0) 59 647 3278

Sweetbank Farm, Co. Wicklow
Homegrown soft fruit
Tel: 00 353 (0) 1 281 9286

Ballylagan Organic Farm, Co. Antrim
Organic fruit and vegetables
Tel: 00 44 (0) 28 9332 867

Helen's Bay Organic Farm, Co. Down
Organic vegetables and fruit
Tel: 00 44 (0) 28 9185 3122

**Culdrum Organic Farm, Co.
Londonderry**
Organic vegetables, pork, chickens and
eggs
Tel: 00 44 (0) 28 7086 8991
www.culdrum.co.uk

Meat

Aherne's Organic Poultry and Beef
Tel: 00 353 (0) 21 463 1058
E-mail:
ballysimonorganicfarm@eircom.net

Coolroe Farm, Co. Cork
Organic poultry
Tel: 00 353 (0) 26 49961

Caherbeg Free Range Pig Farm,
Rosscarbery, West Cork
Free-range bacon, sausages and ham
Tel: 00 353 (0) 23 48474
www.caherbegfreerange.ie
Try the gold award-winning Free Range Dry
Cure Loin Rashers and silver award-winning
Free Range Dry Cure Streaky Rashers.

Jane Russell's Straight Sausages, Co. Kildare
Variety of pork-flavoured sausages
Tel: 00 353 (0) 45 480 100
straightsausages@eircom.net

Highdell Organic Farm, Co. Meath
Organic pork and free-range eggs
Tel: 00 353 (0) 46 902 4954

Terryglass Organic's
Organic pork and pigs
Tel: 00 353 (0) 909 747 341
E-mail: terryglassorganics@eircom.net

Gubbeen Smoke House, Schull, West Cork
Salamis, bacon, hams, and sausages
Tel: 00 353 (0) 28 27824
www.gubbeen.com

Malone Foods, Co. Monaghan
Cured meats
Tel: 00 353 (0) 42 974 5102
www.malonefoods.ie

Ed Hicks, Dublin
Sausages and bacon
Tel: 00 353 (0) 1 284 2700
E-mail: edhick@eircom.net

Krwaczyk's West Cork Salami's, Schull, West Cork
Salamis, terrines and sausages
Tel: 00 353 (0) 28 28579
E-mail: frankk@ocean.free.net

On The Pigs Backs, The Old English Market, Cork
Terrines and pâtés
Tel: 00 353 (0) 21 427 0232
E-mail: sheridan5@eircom.net

The Irish Bay Tree Company, Co. Leitrim
Terrines and pâtés
Tel: 00 353 (0) 71 916 4579
irishbaytree@eircom.net

Moyallon Foods, Co. Armagh
Wild boar, venison pies, bacon and sausages
Tel: 00 44 (0) 28 3834 9100
www.moyallonfoods.com

Pheasant's Hill Farm Shop, Co. Down
Rare-breed pork, beef and lamb
Tel: 00 44 (0) 28 9187 8470

Finnebrogue Venison, Co. Down
Wild red deer
Tel: 00 44 (0) 28 4461 7525
www.finnebrogue.com

Culdrum Organic Farm, Co. Londonderry
Organic vegetables, pork, chickens and eggs
Tel: 00 44 (0) 28 7086 8991
www.culdrum.co.uk

Keady Mountain Farm, Co. Londonderry
Organic chickens, turkeys, ducks and geese
Tel: 00 44 (0) 28 7776 4157

Moss Brook Farm, Co. Londonderry
Sausages, bacon and hams
Tel: 00 44 (0) 28 7963 3454

Fish & Seafood

Belvelly Smokehouse
Smoked salmon, chicken and bacon
Ummera Smokehouse
Timoleague, West Cork
Tel: 00 353 (0) 23 46644
Ship world wide. Mail order enquiries to
shipping@frankhederman.ie
Tel: 00 353 (0) 21 4811089
Fax: 00 353 (0) 21 481 4323
www.ummera.com
Market days: Midleton (Saturday)
Mahon Point (Thursday) and Cobh (Friday)

Burren Smokehouse, Co. Clare
Smoked organic salmon and mackerel
Tel: 00 353 (0) 65 707 4432

Woodcock Smokehouse, Castletownsend, West Cork
Smoked wild salmon, tuna, kippers
Tel: 00 353 (0) 28 36232
E-mail: sallybarnes@iolfree.ie

On The Wild Side, Castlegregory, Co. Kerry
Irish seaweed-based products
Tel: 00 353 (0) 66 7139028
E-mail: seatoland@hotmail.com
Available at following markets: Dingle on
Friday, Kenmare on Wednesday, Limerick
on Saturday, Fota House in Cork once a
month and the English Market in Cork

Aran Smoked Salmon, Co. Galway
Smoked salmon, mackerel, mussels

West Cork Smokehouse, Bandon, West Cork
Smoked salmon, trout, tuna, haddock, cod,
mackerel, mussels, gravadlax
Tel: 00 353 (0) 87 2809368

The Connemara Smokehouse, Co. Galway
Smoked salmon, mackerel and tuna
Tel: 00 353 (0) 95 23739
www.smokehouse.ie

Kinvara Smokehouse, Co. Galway
Organic smoked salmon and gravadlax
Tel: 00 353 (0) 91 637 489
www.kinvarasmokedsalmon.com

Corry Lane Smokehouse, Co. Mullingar
Smoked mackerel, salmon, eels and trout
Tel: 00 353 (0) 43 76264

Pasta

Iago's, The Old English Market, Cork
Fresh pasta, pestoes and sauces
Tel: 00 353 (0) 21 4277047

Noodle House, Co. Sligo
Organic dried pasta
Tel: 00 353 (0) 71 918 5589

Chocolate

Eve St. Leger, Magazine Road, Cork
Handmade chocolates
Tel: 00 353 (0) 21 434 7781/21 434 7984
E-mail: eve@iol.ie

O'Connaill's Chocolates, Carrigaline, Cork
Handmade chocolates
Tel: 00 353 (0) 21 437 3407

Skelligs Chocolates, Co. Kerry
Handmade chocolates
Tel: 00 353 (0) 66 947 9119
www.skelligschocolate.com

Cocoa Bean Chocolates, Limerick
Artsian chocolates
Tel: 00 353 (0) 61 446 615
www.cocoabeanchocolates.com

Preserved

G's Gourmet Jams, Port Laoise
Seasonal handmade jams
Tel: 00 353 (0) 502 31058
E-mails: gsgourmetjams@eircom.net

Clare Jam Company
Handmade jams
Tel: 00 353 (0) 65 707 4778

Filligan's Jams, Co. Donegal
Handmade jams and chutneys
Tel: 00 353 (0) 74 955 1628

Sonia's Inner Pickle
Caribbean-style pickles and dips
Tel: 00 353 (0) 86 313 1362

The Scullery, Co. Offaly
Relishes and chutneys
Tel: 00 353 (0) 506 22566

Janets Country Fare, Co. Wicklow
Relishes, jams and chutneys
Tel: 00 353 (0) 1 204 1957

Laragh Stuart Food
Preserves, relishes, pestoes, and dips
Tel: 00 353 (0) 1 617 4827

Just Organic, East Cork
Pestoes, sauces and soups
Tel: 00 353 (0) 21 481 2367

Bearna Honey
Pure Irish honey
Tel: 00 353 (0) 59 977 3122

Glenanore Honey, East Cork
Runny pure Irish honey
Tel: 00 353 (0) 21 463 1011

Mileeven Honey, co. Kilkenny
Pure honeys and jams
Tel: 00 353 (0) 51 643 368
www.mileevenfinefoods.com

Off Beat Bottling Company
Chutneys and Jams
Tel: 00 44 (0) 28 9127 1525

Juices

The Little Irish Apple Company, Co. Kilkenny
Apple juice - organic and non
Tel: 00 353 (0) 51 387 109
E-mail: littleapple@eircom.net

The Apple Farm, Co. Tipperary
Apple juice and home fruit
Tel: 00 353 (0) 52 41459
www.theapplefarm.com

Crinnaghtaun Apple Juice
Appe juice
Tel: 00 353 (0) 58 54258
www.irishapplejuice.com

Barnhill Apple Juice, Co. Armagh
Apple juice
Tel: 00 44 (0) 28 3885 1190

Websites for Information on Irish Food

www.slowfoodireland.com
www.bordbia.ie
www.craftbutchers.ie
www.irishseedsavers.ie
www.bridgestoneguides.com
www.routiersireland.com
www.irelandmarkets.ie
www.irishfarmersmarkets.com
www.irishbeekeeping.ie

and me:

www.clodaghmckenna.com

Index

Acknowledgements

Dedication

This book is dedicated to my mum, Irene McKenna. She has worked until the early hours of the morning in my kitchen helping to prepare for the markets and driven me hundreds of miles to attend meetings and cookery demonstrations. But, above all, for never doubting me and for always believing in me. I would never have come this far without her.

Acknowledgements

I would firstly like to thank my agent Deborah McKenna, without her support and vision I would never have got the opportunity to meet the wonderful Jenny Heller (commissioning editor for Collins). The whole team at Collins who have spent hours upon hours making this book into the book that I have dreamt of: my editors Alastair Laing and Lizzy Gray and designers Emma Ewbank and Jeremy Tilston. Jean Cazals, the photographer for this book, is one of the most creative and inspiring people I have ever met, I will be forever thankful for the energy that he put in to this book. And his partner Marie-Ange Lapierre, who cooked all my recipes and made them look so beautiful.

Karen McLaughlin has been my mentor and friend for over 5 years, has guided with me with my writing and many other projects.

My parents Jim and Irene, brothers and sisters Jim, Mairead and Niamh and my cousin Barrie Tyner (who is like my brother!) – thank you for listening to all my worries and helping me so much with creating this book.

Above all, I would like to thank all the producers, farmers' market organisers, food writers, who have given me so much of their time, knowledge, tips and recipes, without them there would be no food culture in Ireland and therefore no book.

Lastly, thank you to Darina Allen for introducing me to her vision for food, Rory O'Connaill for empowering me with cooking skills, and Giana Ferguson for introducing me to Slow Food and always being there for me no matter what.

This paperback edition published in 2009 by Collins

First published in 2006 by
Collins, an imprint of
HarperCollins Publishers Ltd
77-85 Fulham Palace Road
London W6 8JB

www.collins.co.uk

Collins is a registered trademark of HarperCollins Publishers Ltd

Text copyright: Clodagh McKenna, 2006
Photography copyright: Jean Cazals, 2006
Map, page 219 copyright: Collins Bartholomew, Conic Equidistant Projection

12 11 10 09

7 6 5 4 3 2 1

Food Stylist: Marie-Ange Lapierre
Prop Stylist: Sue Rowlands
Designers: Emma Ewbank and Jeremy Tilston
Senior Commissioning Editor: Jenny Heller
Copy-editor: Heather Thomas
Senior Editor: Lizzy Gray
Editor: Alastair Laing

ISBN 978-0-00-728481-8

Colour reproduction by DOT Gradations
Printed and bound by Printing Express, Hong Kong